The Recent Graduate's Guide to Wealth Accumulation

(Second Edition)

(The Road to Riches: What They Don't Teach You in School!)

By Stewart Fleisher

This book is intended to provide guidance in regard to the subject matter covered. It is sold with the understanding that the author and publisher are not herein engaged in rendering legal, accounting, tax, financial, or other professional advice or services. If such services are required, professional assistance should be sought.

Although this book contains many factual statements regarding wealth accumulation, certain portions of this book may be fictional in nature.

Published in February, 2019.

ISBN: 0615960502

ISBN-13: 9780615960500

TABLE OF CONTENTS

Dedications and Comments

This book would not have been possible without the support of my loving wife, Jacqueline, to whom I dedicate this book, together with my children and grandchildren. I hope all of them will benefit not just financially from my experiences, but also emotionally, from the frugality and investment ideas contained in this book. Wealth accumulation is not just about money and things, but also about security and knowing that you, and not your boss or someone else, are in control of your life.

I also would like to thank my many friends and relatives for helping me pursue this endeavor. Their encouragement has been inspirational to me. Special thanks are also given to Dave Glubetich, author of <u>The Monopoly Game</u>, for his ideas and encouragement, and permission to include some of his ideas in my book.

I also thank the many clients whose stories have been included herein. The names and the actual situations have been changed to the extent that any resemblance to an actual person or situation is purely coincidental.

The author is currently planning another edition to this book and would welcome any comments, corrections, and additions the reader wishes to make. You are welcome to write the author at:
RecentGradBook@aol.com

***

Preface

"Wealth Accumulation" – Some readers may be intimidated by those words. Other readers may find discussing money as offensive. If you find those words uncomfortable, then mentally substitute them with "financial security." Think of wealth as a storehouse of value – be it cash, investments, or whatever – that can be used for future purchases.

Some may think this book is about some "get rich scheme." Others may think it is about greed. Neither is correct. This book is about living a financially-comfortable life.

The purpose of this book is to help the recent graduate - whether high school, college, or whatever - lead a fuller and happier life. Although this book addresses mainly wealth accumulation, which most readers would acknowledge could be a significant factor to happiness and security, financial success is merely a slice in the pie of living a full and enjoyable life.

Most recent graduates are in the unique position of seeing their income suddenly increase. Although the principles of wealth accumulation discussed in this book are applicable to anyone, the people who suddenly have a major increase in the income, such as recent immigrants, are in a similar position. Recently married couples are also in a similar position as they embark on combining households and changing their spending habits.

Hence these principals of wealth accumulation may be equally applicable to such couples. To get the most out of this book, both spouses should read this book at about the same time.

How individuals manage that increased income or reduced expenditures will be the key to their future wealth. This book can provide the guiding light to help ordinary people accumulate extraordinary wealth.

Can this book help you? If you have even average education and intelligence, have the ability to read, add, and subtract, and really have the desire to achieve a degree of financial security, you have a very valuable tool in your hands to help you achieve these goals.

Specific knowledge of how to achieve your dreams is certainly helpful and this book attempts to give you at least some of that knowledge. But times vary, locations are different, and new methods of achieving your dreams will develop. Perhaps the greatest value of this book will be to give you the incentive to save and to invest in your future. The average person spends more time planning their next vacation than they do their financial future. Now is the time, while you are fresh out of school, or recently married, to take control of your financial life.

Quiz: Six crows are sitting on a fence. One crow decides to fly away. How many crows are left? If you guessed five crows, you are wrong. There are still six crows on the fence. Deciding to do something and actually doing it are two different things. Reading this book will be informative, but it is actually acting on the principals of wealth accumulation that will make a difference in your life. Stop dreaming and start doing!

My hope is that years from now you will look back and say "I am not sure exactly what I remember from Mr. Fleisher's book, but that book was very influential in my financial success." That would be my greatest reward!

***

Introduction

"Never forget that it takes only one idea to change your life forever."

Opening Thoughts: Daydreaming can be fun. Lean back and think about all the things you would like. Let your imagination run crazy. Perhaps you would like to travel; perhaps own a large new home; perhaps have a fancy car, a vacation home in the mountains or on a lake.

Ok, back to reality! Those dreams are fun, but not very realistic. How can you ever be rich enough to do or have all those things? After all, you are stuck with a 9 to 5 job and every time you save for a rainy day, there's a thunderstorm the next week! Does that sound familiar?

But wait! Let's stop all of that negative thinking long enough to read THE RECENT GRADUATE'S GUIDE TO WEALTH ACCUM-ULATION. So turn off the television, the cell phone, and any other distractions, so you can better absorb the concepts in this book. Pick up a pen and highlighter, and be ready to mark those portions of this book which you feel are most relevant to you or which you would like to refer to periodically.

Most of your dreams can come true, but it is going to take some work on your part. This book can be your road map, if you let it. A great many people who have followed the methods outlined in this book have achieved significant wealth.

As you will see, the best way to make your dreams come true is to stop dreaming and start doing. Yes, dreaming is a form of planning, but only when coupled with action. Knowledge alone - even the knowledge obtained through this book - is not sufficient; it must be coupled with action in order to achieve the American Dream. In this book we will offer you not only the knowledge you need to create wealth, but hopefully also provide the motivation to act. For, you see, effective education is not so much in filling the lantern, as it is in the lighting of the wick.

Not A Recent Graduate? Although this book was written primarily for the recent high school or college graduate, the principles of wealth accumulation revealed in this book are applicable to almost anyone, including the concepts of time management, improving job performance, and maximizing investment returns.

Unfortunately, many other people are already "stuck in their ways", and may find it more difficult to implement some of these principles and it may take longer to see results. Certain principles, such as minimizing expenses, are simply easier to adopt while you are young and just starting out in the world.

The average person will live to be 85 years of age, and what you do during the first 25 years will largely determine your success and happiness during the last 60 years. So the sooner you start implementing these principals, the better.

Not Interested In Accumulating Wealth? This book offers you a happier, simpler way to live. By working toward long-term priorities as opposed to short-term pleasures, you will have a greater chance of achieving the things that are important in your life, whatever those things may be.

The proper allocation of scarce resources, such as time, money, and efforts, can make a difference in anyone's life.

Just Getting Started In Life? So those who are just starting out in developing their careers and spending habits, which would include newlyweds and recent immigrants, have, perhaps, the greatest potential to benefit from this book.

Let's explore each category – recent graduates, newlyweds, and immigrants - and discuss why their unique situations lend themselves to wealth building, if, and that's a big if, they are willing to take responsibility for their own financial success.

Recent Graduates: Recent graduates are in a unique position in that they are in the process of developing spending, savings, and career habits that will determine their level of wealth in the future. Most students, be they high school or college, have had very little of their own income. Many have had to struggle financially. Finally, the big day comes for graduation, and just as important for many, the first day on a decent paying job.

Immigrants: Recent immigrants, too, are often used to living on very little. They have not been raised in an environment where people are trying to impress each other. Most are merely trying to survive. Most of those who live at the poverty level in this country would be enjoying a middle class standard of living in many foreign countries.

Immigrants coming to this country have a definite advantage over the typical person who has been living in poverty in this country. Immigrants are used to conserving their financial and other resources because those resources may be necessary for survival in the coming months.

When you are raised in an agrarian (farm-based) society, conservation is a way of life. The Aesop fable about the Ant and the Grasshopper has real meaning in an agrarian environment, as he who only consumes in summer, starves in winter.

The wage levels in this country, even for a farm worker or janitor, are much greater than in many foreign countries. Thus, immigrants from third world countries, including much of Mexico, find that not only are they able to earn enough to live on, but also they are able to send a considerable portion of their earnings back to relatives in their native country.

Those who brought their families with them find they can live better than in their native countries and still save for the future. Perhaps that explains why illegal immigration has become such a problem in this country.

A hundred years ago people immigrated to the United States for freedom. Today, they immigrate for economic opportunity.

Newlyweds: So why are newlyweds included among those who may benefit most from this book? They, too, occupy a unique position in that they are in the process of developing new spending, savings, and career habits that will determine their level of wealth in the future. Newlyweds may be thinking that this book does not apply to them, but their opportunities to create wealth are in many respects quite similar.

The old saying that "Two can live as cheaply as one" is not quite true, but newlyweds who control their expenditures have an excellent chance of accumulating wealth, just as those couples who seem to compete as to whether the husband or the wife can spend the most are condemned to a life of near poverty (and often divorce!)

Habits: Developing constructive habits early in life is easier than trying to change ingrained habits later on. These constructive habits are more likely to lead to wealth creation. We first form habits; then habits form us. If we do not consciously form good habits, we unconsciously form bad ones. The only way to get rid of a bad habit is to replace it with a good habit. Every successful person has simply formed the habit of doing things that failures dislike doing and will not do.

As a recent graduate, immigrant, or newlywed, you have a distinct advantage over most other Americans. You are starting fresh; the habits you develop in the next few years will determine whether you will be living in debt and in poverty most of your life, or whether you will accumulate significant wealth.

More Freedom Today: We live in a country today that has more freedom (and yes, more taxes and regulations) than ever before. Regardless of the color of your skin, your religious beliefs, your ancestry, your sex or sexual preferences, your height or build, there is more opportunity in this country today than ever before.

Yes, there will always be some injustices in the world, most of which we cannot control, but we can control how we react to them. Don't adopt the victim mentality that has kept so many people from moving forward. Adopt an "I can!" mentality to deal with life's problems.

A Unique Position: When starting fresh as a recent graduate, immigrant, or newlywed, your position is unique in a number of ways:

1. You are suddenly earning far more than you did before, and if you are young, you stand to see the biggest increases in your income during the next decade.

2. What you do with that increased income will determine in part your wealth (your net worth) during the next decade or two.

3. Your expenses in the recent past have generally been far below your new current income. You have not yet adopted the "American Way of Life", which is often reflected in out of control spending and living off credit cards. You have a unique opportunity to control your expenditures.

4. You can embark on an investment strategy that will allow you to earn excellent rates of return, such as by buying your own home, buying rental properties, and even investing in the stock market. We will discuss many of these opportunities in later chapters in this book.

Financial Freedom: Many recent graduates, immigrants, and newlyweds have obtained that goal of "financial freedom" at a relatively young age. Financial freedom, if you are not familiar with that term, means having enough wealth and income to do whatever you want, when you want, because you have sufficient assets and income to be able to do so. As discussed later in this book, such wealth and income are relative to your level of expenses; the lower your expenses, the less wealth it takes to achieve financial freedom.

Haven't Things Changed? This book describes how many people became wealthy during the past few decades, or with respect to Benjamin Franklin, over two hundred years ago. "But," you may say, "A lot of things are different now. Can an average person still start from scratch and become wealthy?"

The answer is a definite YES! Of course, times have changed somewhat; prices of almost everything are higher. But there is more opportunity in America now than ever before.

Startup Companies: Twenty years ago people would say that there will never be another opportunity like the ones Steve Jobs (the founder of Apple Computer) and Bill Gates (the founder of Microsoft) had, where they literally started those companies in a garage. Since then, Facebook, Amazon, Twitter, and a slew of other startup companies have created fortunes for their founders, and even small fortunes for many of their early employees. The story about the retired secretary who had worked at Intel most of her life and retired with $6 million of Intel stock is true!

Real Estate: A friend of mine purchased a house in foreclosure for $200,000, fixed it up in his spare time, and sold it two years later for $325,000. He made over $100,000 in two years, and what's most amazing is, he purchased it with only $10,000 down! Furthermore, because he lived in it during those two years while fixing it up, he was able to exclude all of that gain from taxation! For those who get out there and do their homework (not only reading this book, but also acting on it), the accumulation of wealth is almost a certainty!

The Secrets Of Wealth Accumulation: There are many different roads to wealth, but many of those roads are built on the same foundation. Are these secrets that the wealthy refused to share? Not at all. It may surprise you to learn that there really are no secrets. Thousands of people from every walk of life are using these concepts each year to accumulate wealth. And you can too.

This book attempts to assemble much of that sound advice in one place. Benjamin Franklin attempted to do so in his book, "The Way to Wealth", which was a compilation of the wisdom from his "Poor Richard's Almanac." That book and Benjamin Franklin's autobiography have had a strong impact on the lives of many successful people, and both books are recommended to anyone interested in wealth accumulation.

Even a slow reader can read each book in only a few hours. Both books are available through Amazon, your local bookstore, or, if you want to save some money, probably through your local library!

The reader is urged to read other books to discover more on each of the topics discussed in this book. You see, education is not so much in seeking the answers to the questions asked as it is in finding the answers to the questions unasked.

Use not only the brains you have, but also the brains of others. Learn not only from what others have done right, but also learn from their mistakes. You will never live long enough to make all those mistakes yourself.

Action Required: This book offers sound advice that has withstood the test of time. This book could be your short cut to wealth. I can give you counsel, but cannot give you conduct. This book offers a full loaf of bread of advice. Some readers will eat only a few slices, others the whole loaf. But even eating only a few crumbs is better than fasting. Read this entire book. You will never learn that which you do not want to know.

Why This Book Was Written: In my own research of literature to help my own children and others, I found very few books that honestly and objectively discuss the accumulation of wealth in this country. Yes, there are many good books on "Getting out of Debt", "Getting a better Job", "How to be a Successful Manager", or "Investing in Real Estate or the Stock Market", but none of them tied it all together in terms of wealth creation. The author has borrowed many ideas from others. Hopefully, these ideas have been uniquely related to the topic of wealth accumulation in a manner that others have neglected.

Moreover, many such books are written from a very subjective point of view. For instance, a stockbroker writing a book on investing is obviously going to have a propensity to discuss only stocks, and to emphasize the positive aspects while minimizing the negative aspects. If the only tool you have is a hammer, every problem looks like a nail.

Starting With Nothing May Be An Asset: How does one start with nothing, yet accumulate significant wealth? We all came into life with nothing, not even with clothes on our back! Some people become successful in spite of adversity; they rise to the occasion and beat the odds. They rise to upper middle class, and might even be classified as wealthy, while others with seemingly great advantage, raised in middle class families, well educated, not only fail to achieve their potential, but become financial burdens on their families and society.

Many people have immigrated to this country, some from as close as Mexico, some from as far away as Vietnam, Russia, or China. Many came with nothing but the clothes on their back; some came alone; most came with families. Many became middle class; some upper middle class, and a few, wealthy.

Many accomplished these financial feats within ten to twenty years of arriving in this country. Many who rose from abject poverty to middle class have seen their children go on to become very successful and comparatively wealthy.

On the other hand, many American parents who were born here complain that their children not only spend more than they make, but they are constantly relying on them to bail them out of financial difficulties. As one mother put it, "It used to be that having children was an economic asset rather than an economic liability!"

Use Of Wealth: Material wealth can (and should) be used to help others, to help your community, and mankind in general. The author has no quarrel with Warren Buffett who has indicated he plans to leave his great wealth to charity. Having acquired great wealth gives Mr. Buffett options he wouldn't have without it.

One person may spend much of his wealth on educating his children or grandchildren to help give them a head start in life. Another person may decide to retire early and enjoy the fruits of his labor. Another may start a business that employs many people and, in effect, helps him (and them) have a better life. Another person may ultimately donate much of their wealth to their church.

Wealth For Wealth's Sake: Many will do good things with their wealth; a few will do bad things. What you do with your wealth is up to you. In this book I will not offer alternatives or lecture on what should, or should not, be done with wealth once achieved. In a free society, each person has that choice. The primary goal of this book is to guide the reader on the right path toward wealth accumulation.

Many will condemn this book as being materialistic, but may grudgingly accept this book as being the primary way most Americans achieve material wealth. The author wishes to emphasize that, although this book is about accumulating wealth, he does not feel that the accumulation of wealth solely for wealth's sake should be one's sole purpose in life.

On the other hand, there will be many who read this book, acknowledge the wisdom herein, approve of the methodology employed, and immediately practice the contrary. It is only human nature to think wisely and act foolishly. The author accepts that, and realizes that few will practice all espoused in this book.

Sometimes good advice for many may not be applicable to a few. Use what you can to improve your life. If even a few of the principles of wealth accumulation rub off on the reader, the author will feel the effort to create this book has been worthwhile.

Benjamin Franklin: One person whom I interviewed for this book stated, "I was greatly influenced by the 'Autobiography of Benjamin Franklin.' Franklin was one of the most fascinating people in American history. He arrived in Philadelphia almost penniless, and after apprenticing for several years, built up the most profitable printing business in the American colonies, franchising his system in the other colonies."

"Franklin went on to become not only wealthy, but also famous in politics, in science, and in philanthropy. Quotes from his publication, "Poor Richard's Almanac" (for example, 'A penny saved is a penny earned') and his constantly emphasizing thrift in his autobiography made a lasting impression on me. I grew up frugal, though nowhere near as frugal as Mr. Franklin. Whenever I received a gift of money, a cash bonus, or even my regular paycheck, my thoughts were on what saving it might mean in the future, rather than what I could enjoy by spending it in the present."

"My cousin grew up as a profligate, and will probably never have much wealth. He still rents an apartment because he cannot afford the down payment on a house. I have offered to help him with the down payment if he could qualify for a loan, but because of his large credit card debt, part of which he has been late in paying, he is unable to obtain a mortgage loan. I think he will die poor."

Disadvantaged? Maybe That Is An Asset! Why is it that some people, poor and comparatively uneducated, suffering from great disadvantage, are able to achieve not only economic success, but in many cases accumulate significant wealth?

What sets these persons apart from the "economically disadvantaged Americans," equally poor, who become a liability to society? What sets these persons apart from the privileged-class, college-educated kid who can never seem to hold a job and yet who overspends when he or she is employed?

In this book we will try to explore the habits of those who have become successful and compare them with the habits of those who fail to live up to their potential.

Just as I have observed immigrants who, with low paying jobs, accumulate significant wealth, I have also observed corporate executives who once earned over $500,000 per year, and who within a few years after their jobs disappeared, were living off credit cards and were virtually bankrupt. Their income, though great, never materialized into net worth because of their high level of expenditures.

Learn From Others: You will never live long enough to learn everything that you need to know to succeed in life, especially on your own. That's why reading about the success or failure of others is so important.

As one observer put it, "It is not only more efficient to learn from the mistakes of others, but it is also less expensive than learning from your own experience! Wise men learn much from other's mistakes; fools barely learn from their own."

Failure As An Asset? Don't let the fear of making a mistake discourage you from taking the actions suggested in this book. He who never makes a mistake, never makes a discovery. If you have never failed, you have never tried anything new. Consider a few of these "failures":

Albert Einstein: He wasn't able to speak until he was 4 years old and his teachers said he "would never amount to much."

Walt Disney: He was fired from a newspaper job because he "lacked imagination and had no original ideas."

Oprah Winfrey: She was demoted from her job as a news anchor because "she wasn't fit for television."

The Beatles: Decca Recording Studios rejected them, saying "We don't like their sound. They have no future in show business."

Steve Jobs: At 30 years old, he was left devastated and depressed after being unceremoniously fired from the company (Apple) he had started.

Michael Jordan: After being cut from his high school basketball team, he went home, locked himself in his room, and cried.

Television – An Asset Or A Liability? Television can be a great source of knowledge and motivation, but for most people, it is solely a source of temporary enjoyment, with no lasting value. Arnold watches only shows on the lives of successful people, such as biographies on Bill Gates, Warren Buffet, Thomas Edison, Henry Ford, and even George Bush and Barrack Obama. Justin only watches sitcoms and popular movies. Who do you think is more likely to be successful?

To a great extent, we become what we feed our minds. For Justin, it's garbage in, garbage out. As Ann Landers puts it: "Television is proof that married couples will look at anything rather than each other." But television has the potential to be a motivating force if properly used.

As William Paley (the former president of CBS) once said of television, "Don't blame the tool; blame the workman for how he uses it."

For decades the typical American has been exposed to a constant bombardment of advertisements on television and elsewhere that stress spending. He has developed the habit of responding to those ads. Not one ad in a thousand stresses wealth accumulation. And if "saving" is even ever mentioned, it is usually in terms of "buy today and save!"

Time Is Money: Never say you don't have enough time; you have exactly the same number of hours each day that were given to Albert Einstein, Thomas Jefferson, Leonardo da Vinci, Bill Gates, and Thomas Edison.

The degree of your success will be determined by what you do with those hours. Hint: Get up 30 minutes early each day. Doing this each day for one year will give you the equivalent of two extra weeks to accomplish the important things in your life. Do it for 26 years and it will add an extra year to your working life.

Don't waste time, for it is the substance from which life is made. Lost time is never found again. If you have something you should do tomorrow, do it today. Time management is so important that I have devoted several chapters in this book to that subject. One chapter is entitled, "The $100,000 idea!" That idea alone has made many people far more productive and efficient in their everyday life.

Keep An Open Mind: You do not have to adopt all the strategies in this book. You will deviate, unexpected developments will steer you off-course, and unexpected expenses will appear. It has been stated that the average American has unexpected expenses every month of his life, but does not plan to have any during the next year!

Nor do I espouse dedicating your life to accumulating wealth to no end. Assign priorities to the expenditures that are really important to you. Avoid, or at least minimize, expenditures that do not have a high priority and use both your money and your time wisely.

Life Is Like A Game Of Cards. The hand you are dealt is pre-determined; the way you play it is your own free will. If you never attempt to do what you do not think you can do, you will never accomplish all that you can do.

What is important today is not where you stand, but the direction you are heading. Judge not each day by the harvest you reap, but by the seeds you plant.

To quote "Through the Looking Glass" by Lewis Carroll: One day Alice came upon a fork in the road and saw a Cheshire cat in a tree. "Which road should I take?" asked Alice. "That depends on where you want to go," replied the cat. "I don't care," answered Alice. "Then," said the cat, "It doesn't matter which road you take."

Set Your Goals: The first step to getting the things you want out of life is this: Decide what it is that you want. The creation of wealth makes many of those things possible. And that is the reason why the "creation of wealth" has been a major goal of successful people.

Absorb what you can from this book. You can achieve significant wealth if you put your mind to it.

A State Of Mind: When it comes to becoming wealthy, whether you think you can or you think you can't, you are right. Achievement is largely a state of mind. Yes, there will be obstacles along the way, but nothing would ever be attempted if all possible obstacles must first be removed.

One inspiring poet put it this way:

> If you think you are beaten, you are.
> > If you think you dare not, you don't.
> If you'd like to win but you think you can't,
> > It's almost a cinch you won't.
> If you think you'll lose, you're lost.
> > For out in the world we find,
> Success begins with the fellow's will,
> > It's all in the state of mind.
> If you think you're outclassed, you are;
> > You've got to think high to rise,
> You've got to be sure of yourself before
> > You can ever win a prize.
> Life's battles don't always go
> > To the stronger or faster man;
> But sooner or later the man who wins
> > Is the man who thinks he can.

Yes, there will be sacrifices. But ask people who on their own have accumulated significant wealth if it was worth it, and virtually all of them will say that it was.

So what is wealth? How is it created? These are questions answered in the next chapter.

***

What is "Wealth"?

"Wealth is not having all the money you want, but having all the money you need."

What Is Wealth? Dollars earned but unspent constitute the storage of wealth. Wealth is spending power saved up for the future, deferred spending, if you will. Wealth is economic security.

My reference in this book to wealth is not a life-style, a spending pattern, or even a level of income. Perhaps the best measure of wealth is your net worth. While many readers may think of their "net worth" in terms of their value to the community and their family, in this book we refer to net worth as an accounting concept: Assets (what you own) minus Liabilities (what you owe). If you have assets of $20,000 and liabilities of $5,000, your net worth is $15,000.

Note that if you were to pay off your liabilities with part of your assets, your net worth would, at that moment in time, remain the same: $15,000 of assets and no liabilities.

Nevertheless, over time such repayment is likely to impact your net worth. For instance, let's assume you were earning 5% on your assets, but paying 15% on your liabilities (credit cards.) Had you not paid off those liabilities, the interest cost on the liabilities (15% of $5,000, or $750) would have exceeded your income on the savings (5% of $5,000, or $250) by $500 for the year.

Stated another way, your net worth increased by $500 per year by repaying the loan when compared to if you hadn't repaid it.

The difference is actually greater, because the income earned on the asset is probably taxable, whereas the interest on the liability (such as credit cards) is not deductible!

Periodic Assessment: It has been observed that successful people calculate their net worth at least annually to keep track of where they stand with respect to their financial goals. Doing so is relatively simple: Simply list everything you own, all your assets and their values. Then list all your debts (liabilities). The difference is your net worth. All assets and liabilities should be valued as of a particular date, such as December 31.

But even this measure of net worth can be misleading, because wealth is not a specific number. It is a level of comfort. For wealth should be measured against your level of expenditures, both current and future levels. One excellent measure of wealth is the length of time you could live off your investments if you stopped working today. In this regard, wealth is a measure of security.

Who's More Wealthy? A few examples may be helpful to demonstrate this concept. David's net worth (assets less liabilities) is $200,000. Joe's net worth is only $120,000. Joe is a painting contractor. He and his wife earn $60,000 per year, but spend only $40,000. If Joe and his wife were to stop working, their net worth could pay for their living expenses for three years. David earns $200,000 per year, but spends all of his earnings. If he lost his job, his net worth would cover his expenditures for only one year.

David certainly earns more than Joe, spends more, and has a greater net worth. But who is wealthier? While I won't answer that question at this point, I will point out that in terms of economic security, Joe is certainly more secure. I will also ask another question of the reader. Who is likely to have a greater net worth ten years from now?

Stanley Schoolteacher is another person who has accumulated a certain degree of wealth without accumulating significant "net worth", or investments. Stanley has had a rewarding teaching career and has helped many students go on to college and achieve their own levels of success. Based on that alone, one could view Stanley as a success, but not necessarily wealthy, at least by our definition. But let's look more closely at Stanley's situation.

Stanley recently retired from teaching in the public school system, and now teaches part-time at a private school. Although the salary he earned at the public school far exceeded his current salary, Stanley's retirement pension is $3,000 per month and he will receive this pension for the rest of his life and with annual cost of living increases. Stanley is 60 years of age and likely to live to 85 years of age. (Yes, the average life expectancy for a healthy 60 year old is over 25 years!)

If Stanley does live another 25 years, he will receive more than one million dollars in retirement pay with cost of living increases! Viewed another way, had Stanley not had this pension, he would have had to accumulate $600,000 of assets invested at 6% to give him the $3,000 per month that he now receives from the pension. Let's review that math: $600,000 times 6% equals $36,000 per year. $36,000 per year divided by twelve months equals $3,000 per month.

Thus, compared to the person without such a pension, Stanley is comparatively wealthy. In calculating your net worth, you may wish to consider such things as pensions and other benefits that your employment may offer.

Investment Returns: Larry has investments of $300,000 in investments earning 3%, or $9,000 per year. Kim's investments of only $250,000 are invested in a number of stocks that are expected to earn 8% or $20,000 per year. Who is wealthier?

Larry has more savings, but those savings generate less investment income. Certainly in terms of net worth, Larry is wealthier. But who do you think will be wealthier in 10 to 20 years?

Watch For Opportunities: "Opportunity only knocks once." That expression is most often used by someone trying to sell you something. But sometimes exceptional opportunities do appear and are worth taking advantage of. You need to be the one who recognizes and evaluates such opportunities.

For instance, in 1975 a young Harvard man faced a difficult decision. His school experiences gave him an inside edge in working with new technological products. He feared that if he stayed in college, he might miss the opportunity to fully develop his potential in this field. The young man dropped out of Harvard to write software for microcomputers. You may have heard of that young man. His name is Bill Gates, the founder of Microsoft.

Bill Gates is an exceptional success story. But a good business idea, coupled with hard work, has led many to wealth creation over a period of years. For instance, Mark Zuckerberg also dropped out of Harvard to found Facebook!

The Top 1%: Bill Gates, Jeff Bezos, and Mark Zuckerberg are, of course, wealthy by any measure. Another 1% of the households in America today have a net worth of well over one million dollars! Furthermore, there are millions of other Americans who have achieved a comfortable degree of wealth.

People often ask: How can I, starting with nothing, accumulate significant wealth? Unfortunately, everybody is looking for the fast solution, the quick fix.

No Quick Fix: Let's examine a few of these: "I'm gonna be a rock star!" (Movie star, sports star, you name it). Rock stars, sports stars, movie stars, and other entertainers seem to achieve overnight success." That's a common misconception.

Ray Charles once told a reporter that he played in honkytonks, enduring racial slurs, for over fifteen years before he became "an overnight success."

For every wealthy entertainer, for every wealthy football player, there are thousands, many equally talented, who never succeeded. Perhaps they never got the breaks. Perhaps they didn't have the personality. But unless you are extremely talented AND extremely motivated AND extremely lucky, you have very little chance of becoming an economic success in those fields. Better stick with your day job!

Another Observation: The easier the fortune comes, the faster it goes. There are countless stories of successful entertainers being broke, some even in bankruptcy, after just a few years. Some mismanage their finances; others lose much to friends and drugs. Few remain wealthy after their career fades.

Marry Into Money: "You can marry more money in ten minutes than you can earn in a lifetime." There certainly is an element of truth in that statement. But marrying into money comes with additional emotional baggage that can cause tremendous stress in your life.

First, the creator of the wealth, be it your spouse or your spouse's parents, will never think you are "good enough" for your spouse. You will be under the microscope. If your spending/saving habits don't coincide with the creator's habits while developing that wealth, your marriage is likely to be either miserable or short-lived.

The secret to living successfully with money into which you marry is to adopt the spending, saving, working, and investing habits of the creator of that wealth had when starting out. Inquire how he or she developed that wealth. That tip could be extremely valuable to you, both with your financial life as well as with your married life.

To a large degree how in-laws evaluate you is subjective. There is an old joke about a mother describing her two children: "Oh, my daughter, she is married to a wonderful man. She doesn't have to work. She can stay at home all day and watch TV or go shopping. She doesn't even have to cook as he takes her out for dinner almost every night. Oh, but my son! He is married to the laziest girl I have even seen. She won't get a job. All she does all day is watch TV and shop, and she doesn't even cook, so he has to take her out for dinner almost every night."

The "wealth creator" is more than likely dissatisfied with one or more of his or her children. As an in-law, you are starting at even a greater disadvantage.

Inherited Wealth: It's easier to inherit money than to earn it! It's also true that you can inherit more money in ten minutes than you can earn in a lifetime. Perhaps you have already inherited a small fortune or know that you are likely to in the future.

One commentator has observed that if the recipient was not heavily involved in the creation of that wealth, he or she is likely to squander it. For those who inherit an estate, of which they know not of the labor that went into obtaining such wealth, are seldom concerned about conserving such wealth. They spend a little today, and a little more the next day. It's like drinking water from a bucket, and never putting any more in. Sooner or later, the water runs out and the drinker knows not of the well where more can be obtained.

Study after study confirms that inherited money is usually dissipated within only a few years. Benny was a twenty-one year old student when he inherited over $500,000. He dropped out college and within five years the inheritance was all gone. So at 26 years of age, he had no college degree, no work history, and was now looking for his first job. Frankly, Benny's life would have been better had his parents left his inheritance to charity!

The Lottery: Many people feel that winning the lottery would change their lives, and it might, sometimes for the better, but often for the worse. We frequently hear of big lottery winners who are destitute in just a few years. Again, if you didn't earn it, you are not likely to keep it.

A wealthy client once explained to me that he was glad there was a lottery. He put it this way: "The lottery is basically a tax on the poor. The government typically keeps 50% of what gamblers bet.

That means that for every $10 you spend every week, you will "win" - on average - only $5. Therefore, it is a voluntary tax that I have elected not to pay by not buying a ticket. The more money the government makes on the lottery, the less the government needs to tax me!"

Statistics bear out that most lottery tickets are purchased by poor people. Many feel that is the only way out of poverty. As long as they feel that way and keep buying lottery tickets, the vast majority will remain in poverty. The time spent looking for a "quick fix" would better be spent concentrating on the proven wealth accumulation techniques.

If you really must have the dream of winning the lottery, recognize the realities, and buy just one ticket per month.

One of my favorite stories is of Joe sitting alone in church, praying "Oh, Lord, please let me win the lotto! Please let me win the lotto." Then there is lightning and thunder, and a deep voice comes from the top of the church, "I'd like to help you, Joe, but first you have to buy a ticket!" If the Lord really wants you to win, one ticket per month should suffice.

A billboard in front of another church says: "Sermon today: The Evils of Gambling!" and at the bottom is: "Don't miss Bingo on Tuesday night!" Funny how churches and governments can rationalize the legitimacy of gambling when they can make a profit off it! Remember, that profit is at your expense!

Wealth Benefits Others: Wealth is one of our basic human desires. Wealth has attracted many negative comments, such as money can't buy happiness, but also many positive observations, "Don't knock the rich - When did a poor person ever give you a job?"

Is Wealth Evil? Many will criticize wealth as evil. They will mis-quote the Bible: "Money is the root of all evil." The actual quote is, "The Love of money is the root of all evil." But the creation of wealth is not focused on the love of money; it's focused on the accumulation of money by providing services that society is willing to pay for; by living the frugal life, not conspicuous spending beyond your means, and investing for the greatest returns.

Is the person who saves his money to pay cash for the things he wants in the future any more "evil" than the person who spends his money before he earns it by financing the purchases with credit card debt?

Security: Wealth also equates to security. With considerable savings and investments, if you lose your job, if you have a major unexpected expenditure, you are not forced into expensive borrowing.

Who is more likely to commit a crime, the person who has a net worth of one million dollars, or the person who is desperately in debt?

Motivation: How and why do you develop a burning desire to be wealthy? Why such a desire is important should be obvious; few people develop significant wealth without a plan, a goal in mind.

If you have no desire to be wealthy, you probably never will be. You need to have a burning desire, a level of hunger that will provide the moving force that excites, motivates, and propels you.

Interestingly, when you are focused on where you are going, you burn the least amount of energy to get there.

Numbers are a road map to wealth. They are the primary measure of knowing if you are on course. To make quality decisions, you need quality numbers. Money grows as a result of two forces, Time and Rate. That's another reason to set your goals early; you have more time to accumulate that wealth.

You can learn as much from others about what they did wrong as what they did right. You will make many mistakes as you achieve significant wealth. They won't destroy you unless they destroy your motivation. Wise men learn from their mistakes. Seldom can one accumulate wealth without riding a roller coaster along the way.

The Path To Wealth: The way to wealth for most people is as plain as the nose on your face. It depends chiefly on three concepts: maximizing income, minimizing expenses, and profitably investing the difference.

This book has chapters dealing with all three topics, reducing expenditures, maximizing income, and maximizing investment returns. The order discussed is not important, but I chose minimizing expenditures to be first as that's the one aspect of wealth accumulation over which the average person can exert the most control, or, as I have observed of late, the aspect over which some people exert the least control - to their ultimate financial detriment.

Before we explore minimizing expenses, the next chapter will discuss the difference between "Being Cheap" and "Being Frugal."

***

Cheap versus Frugal

"They are quite different!"

Before we discuss "minimizing expenses" in any detail, we think it is important to distinguish between Cheap and Frugal.

Cheap vs. Frugal: Cheap is a derogatory term often used to describe people who are so restrictive in their spending habits that they take advantage of other people. Cheap infers miserly or stingy.

By contrast, frugal people are those who are careful in their spending on themselves, those who are looking for a good deal or not spending money at all. The frugal person economizes in spending his own resources by depriving himself of something he may personally want.

A person who goes to an expensive restaurant, has a $150 meal and then leaves the waiter a $5 tip, is not frugal, but is cheap. A person who goes to an inexpensive restaurant, splits a meal with his wife, drinks water, and then leaves the waitress a 20% tip is not cheap, but is frugal.

Neither Involves Dishonesty: All too often people confuse frugality, or even cheapness, with those who would steal or otherwise take something that isn't theirs or that they are not entitled to. The person who puts 20 "Sweet and Low" packages in his pocket at a restaurant is neither cheap nor frugal, but is dishonest. Although the restaurant offers "Sweet and Low" at no additional charge to those who wish to use it in their drink, they do not offer it free to anyone who wants to carry it out of the restaurant.

The person who doesn't finish his meal and then takes home the rest of his meal is frugal. The person who enjoys five cups of coffee when the restaurant offers free refills is neither cheap nor dishonest, but is frugal. He has accepted an offer extended by the restaurant. But the person who pays for a cup of coffee that does not offer free refills, but then refills his cup without paying, is neither frugal, nor cheap, but dishonest.

The person who seeks four bids before having his house painted, then negotiates the low bidder to reduce his price even further, is frugal. Cheap involves limiting your expenditures at other people's expense.

The person who contracts to have his house painted, then complains about every imperfection, trying to renegotiate the price for work which was reasonably completed, is cheap. The person who refuses to pay the contractor is dishonest.

The Spendthrift: A spendthrift is a person who spends money imprudently or wastefully, and often far beyond his or her means. Ironically, a person can be a spendthrift with respect to himself, and cheap with respect to others.

Frugality: Being frugal is the opposite of being a spendthrift. A frugal person spends his money wisely. Frugality involves limiting expenditures at your own sacrifice. Do you really need a new sweater or will the one from last winter do? The person who doesn't buy that new sweater is frugal. If a new sweater really is needed, the person who shops at the thrift store is being frugal. The person who sees a sweater in a catalog at a high price (after all, it is a "famous brand!") and then orders it - often without even thinking about if it is really needed and obviously not trying it on - is a spendthrift.

Are you starting to see the picture? When we speak of limiting your expenditures in this book, we are not advocating doing that which is dishonest. We are advocating getting good value for your dollar. We are talking about not spending money unless it is absolutely necessary.

We are talking about finding a less expensive way to purchase goods and services. And, yes, sometimes we are talking about settling for lower quality when the lower price justifies it. Do you really need a high quality winter overcoat when you only wear it a few times a year? Do you really need a Rolex watch, when a Timex watch keeps time nearly as well? Do you really need to fly first class when a coach seat on the same plane will get you to your destination at the same time, but at one-third of the cost?

Quality: Many people like to say that they will not compromise on quality. That sure sounds good. But in reality, we all made decisions every day that involve compromises with respect to price and quality.

We usually know the exact price of two items, but we seldom can accurately measure the quality of two items, and even if the quality could be measured, that difference in quality may have different values to different people.

Many purchases are based upon the image we wish to project and not about absolute quality. Nobody buys a Rolex watch because it keeps time with 99.999% accuracy versus a Timex with keeps time with only 99.91% accuracy. Often it is our concern about image, our vanity, which keeps us from accumulating wealth.

Yes, we all made mistakes occasionally when compromising on quality. The person buying the lowest price item will probably make more mistakes than the person buying the highest price item.

But would you rather make two mistakes buying a $10 item or one mistake buying a $100 item?

Cheap Quality Defined: The word cheap can also be used to derogatorily refer to the quality of an item. A "cheap" watch is one that does not keep good time, or if it does, does so only for a few months. A "cheap" shirt is one that shrinks, one that loses its buttons, one that fades rapidly, and one whose stitches come loose the first month. A similar shirt without these flaws would not be categorized as being cheap, but as being a good buy if reasonably price, but would be a poor buy if overpriced when compared to similar shirts of similar quality.

Miserly: Miserly refers to someone who hoards money solely for money's sake. Many people who are frugal are not miserly. A frugal person who contributes his fair share to his church and community is not miserly. One can be frugal and still be a contributor to the community.

Selfishness: Frugality is not the same as selfishness. The father who buys a new tie he does not need, and then tells his son they can't afford the baseball glove the son needs for little league, is selfish - not frugal.

The Law Of Diminishing Returns: Deciding how frugal to be often turns on what is called the law of diminishing returns. On a hot summer day, an ice cream cone may offer great satisfaction. The second ice cream cone offers additional pleasure, but probably not as much as the first cone. The third and fourth cones offer even less. The fifth cone may actually make you sick. This concept of diminishing pleasure with the second, third, or fourth purchase applies to many of our day-to-day purchases. We cannot wear more than one pair of shoes at a time, but we may need more than one pair if needed for different uses. But do we really need six pairs of tennis shoes?

Not Just Money: Frugality is not just about money. A person can be frugal about how he spends his time. He spends it wisely. A person can be frugal about he uses his mind. He uses it wisely.

Economize: In this book we are not advocating being dishonest or even being cheap, but being careful about your expenditures. Economizing is perhaps a better word. We all have a limited amount of money and a limited amount of time. Using both wisely makes sense. Most people who have accumulated a significant amount of wealth have done so by being careful with their expenditures by properly evaluating the trade-offs between price and quality.

Long-Term Goals: The decisions you make with respect to such purchases may well determine if you have the money for other purchases which perhaps should have a higher priority, such as accumulating enough funds for the down payment on a house, or a comfortable retirement, or education for your children. What are your long term goals and how should those goals impact your immediate spending goals? Only you can answer that question.

Yes, you can "afford" to buy the extra pairs of tennis shoes, but at what ultimate cost? The person who wears expensive jewelry and drives an expensive car, and then complains about not being able to afford the down payment on a home, has simply made the choice that the jewelry and the car were more important to him or her than owning a home. He who will not economize will someday agonize.

Standard Of Living: So does a frugal person necessarily compromise on his standard of living? Not necessarily. The person who turns off the lights, turns down the thermostat in the winter, buys only one or two pairs of tennis shoes, wears little or no jewelry, drives an older (but reliable) car, does not necessarily enjoy a lower standard of living.

Does that same person who later purchases a home then have a higher standard of living than the person who was less "frugal" but then can't afford a home?

Current vs. Future Spending: Wealth accumulation for most people usually involves making those difficult decisions between current spending and future spending. Most people who want to ultimately purchase a home, send their children to college, have a comfortable retirement, or help their church, must necessarily decide in favor of spending less today so they will have more to meet their long term goals in the future.

Money is a storehouse of value, the value of which can be enjoyed immediately or enjoyed in the future. The accumulation of this storehouse of value will give you more options in the future. Being frugal today may even give you the option of spending more foolishly in the future, if you so desire. Everybody loves a bargain, but even a bargain priced "below cost" is not a bargain if we really don't need it. Is the super buy on the $150 tennis shoes really more important to your long term goals than, say, buying a home? A dollar spent foolishly is forever lost.

Poverty: Don't confuse being frugal with living in poverty. Many people find that, after being frugal, they actually enjoy their station in life more than the person who spends foolishly. There is a certain virtue in living the frugal life. Frugal persons often realize how little they need to make them happy.

Madison Avenue (a term used to refer to the mass advertising industry) has tried for decades to convince us that the latest car, the latest computer, suit, shampoo - you name it - will make us happier.

Frugal people are able to resist such subtle persuasions, realizing that material goods are not the key to happiness. Relationships with friends and family, community involvement, your health, are all often more important.

Frugality Is Reversible! Another interesting thing about frugality: A frugal person can always decide at a later date to buy that item he decided not to buy. But the person who has purchased the item can very rarely make the decision to reverse the purchase. Buying an item is a one-way street, whereas being frugal and not buying the item offers the option later on of either buying the item or using the money for a different purchase that has a higher priority.

Family: Frugality also impacts those you live with, sometimes positively, sometimes negatively. The old saying is that frugal people are hell to live with, but great to have as ancestors! It has been said that a marriage between a frugal person and a spendthrift won't last long. But both can be a positive influence on each other. The spendthrift's spending habits may be reduced, while the frugal person can be kept from becoming cheap. Children often complain how frugal their parents are, but then those children grow up to be just like their parents, confirming that frugality is a habit worth nourishing.

The Future Of Frugality: In this age of consumerism, is frugality becoming old fashioned? No, but its popularity is cyclical. There was a definite resurgence during the "Great Recession" (lasting from 2008 through 2012). During that time frugality found a new following. Facing financial uncertainty, less job security, and the decrease in retirement investments, many people suddenly embraced frugality.

Thrift stores, dollar stores, and rummage/garage sales experienced a resurgence of interest. As people were laid off and tried to keep their home from going into foreclosure, setting spending priorities resulted in much greater acceptance of frugality.

Unfortunately with the economic recovery, interest in frugality has waned. Nevertheless, those who practice it can still accumulate significant savings while still maintaining a reasonable lifestyle.

Unemployment: As the saying goes, "A recession is when your neighbor is laid off; a depression is when you are laid off." Austerity became necessary for the unemployed to survive. Even those employees who were not laid off, no longer had the urge to "keep up with the Joneses." In fact, if "Jones" was unemployed, his (or her) neighbors felt guilty flaunting their current employment status, and actually mimicked Jones's sudden frugality.

The neighbors heard how Jones lost his home in foreclosure because his unemployment check was barely enough to pay his minimum credit cards payments. His neighbors no longer went into debt to pay for things that they don't have the money to pay for. Hearing about the trouble Jones had made them realize the importance of saving for a rainy day. The easiest way to do so is to reduce expenses or never incur such expenses to begin with.

The Economy vs. You: But isn't "spending" good for the economy? Our government from time to time has urged us to spend, like right after the 9-11 terrorist attack. Other times, like during World War II, it urged us to save, and touted, "Buy U.S. Savings Bonds!"

But what if everyone adopted a frugal approach to life? Wouldn't that be bad for the economy? In the short run, perhaps, but with greater wealth later on, there would actually be more spending. Arguing that being frugal, which might be best for you, would devastate the economy makes as much sense as not buying toilet paper, because if everybody ran out and bought toilet paper that would create a shortage of toilet paper. The "might be bad for the economy" argument is simply a feeble excuse to engage in foolish spending.

Regardless of what may be good for the economy, you have got to look out for what is good for you.

Driving your car pollutes the air, but that doesn't mean that you should never drive. Paying taxes helps the government, but that doesn't mean that you should pay all of your income to the government, or that you should even pay more than the law requires. And just because someone (who has something to sell?) says you should spend to help the economy, that shouldn't motivate you to spend any more than you would otherwise spend.

Overspending: It was that "overspending" that caused much of the housing crisis and great recession. How's that, you ask? With rising home values, many people refinanced every couple of years to pull out the equity in their homes. That equity was used to buy new cars, pay off credit card balances which had been run up during the previous year or two, and perhaps, take an expensive vacation.

Moreover, much of what the American public has been buying is illiquid – that is, it cannot be converted to cash without great loss. Houses can be sold, but with a 6% commission. Large screen TVs, computers, and clothes can be sold, but for only a very small fraction of their purchase price.

The Era Of Easy Credit: Easy credit in the 2001-2007 era made borrowing very easy. Credit card offers filled every mailbox and daily emails offered to refinance your mortgage. As a result, by 2008 many people had so much junk in their garage that they had to park their car in the driveway. They had to store the clothes they never wear in the basement because their closets were full.

Only in America do people have to rent a shed in which to store their excess stuff.

People who spend everything they earn are living a life of economic insecurity, making them extremely vulnerable to almost any form of bad luck, such as losing their jobs, their car breaking down, health problems, and the like. A typical response of such people is, "No problem, I just won't make my credit card payments for a few months; then everything will be alright." Of course, that just leads to greater problems in the future. When credit was so easy, it's no wonder that many people felt "Why save? I can just borrow more until I get over the hump."

The Great Recession: Of course, additional borrowing is simply more of the same food that made them sick in the first place. Many people lost a sense of reality and consumed not only every dollar of what they earned, by also every dollar of equity in their home. When the economy tanked in the 2008 to 2010 period, housing prices stopped rising, refinancing wasn't an option, so a great many people were forced to cut back their spending. That, in turn, made the economy even worse, which led to more unemployment, falling home prices, and less "wealth" in the community.

That stuff in the garage that cost over $12,000 now had a liquidation value of less than $1,000. Ditto for the $8,000 paid for the clothes in the basement. These are the same people who lost their job and a year later lost their house to the mortgage company because they had no cash reserves. The government that was there encouraging them to spend, wasn't there to help them when their homes went into foreclosure, or when the credit card companies were suing them.

The Moral: When times are good, don't follow the herd by living beyond your means. Save for lean times. The person who does that doesn't even have to cut back much when times get tough. Living below one's means allows one to keep the same standard of living even when those means suddenly drop.

Defining Yourself: Mass advertising attempts to convince you that your identity is defined by what you own, and not by what you do or by who you are. Moreover, it can be so convincing that many people fall into the trap of thinking that other people will judge them by, not who or what they are, but by what they own.

But the reality is most people eventually realize that owning and consuming does not satisfy that desire to redefine themselves. You are still a loving mother whether you drive a new car or an older car. Which is more important: Being a loving mother or driving a new car?

If you have any doubts, ask your children! (Hint: If they say the new car, then they have been watching too much television!)

If we lack confidence or purpose in our lives, material goods will seldom help. Few people are loved or appreciated because of what the own; love stems from who they are. It is one thing to say that you admire your neighbor's new car (although you probably wouldn't admire his car payments!). It another to say you have to have one just like it (or better.)

The quality of one's life is not measured by the amount of money one can spend, but by the happiness one derives from what one is or has, such as family, friends, and respect. A person with simple needs can be far happier than the spendthrift who relies on consumption in seeking happiness. Reject the idea that who you are is measured by the stuff you own.

Be Your Own Person: "Waste not, want not" is the byline of the frugal person. A frugal person lives on his own terms, and not those of the TV advertisers. Frugal people don't worry about impressing people by having the latest clothes, car, cell phone, or what have you.

Interestingly, when given the opportunity to be around other frugal people, the frugal person will often brag to others with how frugal they are. They might even be smug in how they can resist the temptation to spend money or in the extreme steps they have taken to save money. Frugality is not something to be hidden, but to be proud of.

The Environment: Interestingly, frugal people may actually help with the environmental problems. Frugal people use less energy, drive fewer miles, and contribute less to landfills than their consumption driven counterparts. If you are really concerned about global warming, overflowing landfills, and the ozone layer, simply buy less "stuff." Virtually everything you buy takes energy to make and energy to transport. Being frugal not only reduces your expenses, but also reduces your impact on the environment.

Think of frugality as being "consumer-lite", that is.a simple way to live and not as a severe sacrifice of basic necessities. Other than food, medicine, and perhaps toilet paper, most people have all they need to live basically, and without another purchase for several years.

Entertainment: For many, shopping is not about obtaining necessities, but is a form of entertainment. To some extent, shopping has replaced spending time with family and friends, or even dealing with everyday problems.

Two women were walking out of Macy's department store, both with several full bags. One woman was complaining to the other about that awful bank that was foreclosing on her house. Is that woman under the delusion that buying more stuff that she probably doesn't really need will somehow replace her depression about losing her home? I envision that her husband is similarly buying a new truck on credit because the car salesman pointed out to him that after the foreclosure, his credit would be so poor that he would not qualify to buy a new truck.

Abstinence: Does frugality mean abstinence and deprivation, a life with no pleasures? No, not at all. It's a question of choices. You can get as much pleasure (maybe more) out of taking your child to a free day at the zoo as attending a $150 per ticket concert by Taylor Swift. Buying books you have no time to read can be replaced by trips to the local library. How many people wandering around Barnes and Noble visited their local library first? I'll bet it's close to zero!

A parsimonious life does not have to be a life without pleasure. Ten years from now, which will be more remembered - or even more treasured - the trip to the zoo with your child or the Billy "What's his name" concert? Hiking with friends or a new shirt and matching tie? Visiting a thrift store with friends to see who can find the best bargain, or going to the racetrack to see who can lose the most money?

Extremes: Can frugality be carried to an extreme? Of course, as can most any type of behavior which, when carried to such an extreme, can impact your life adversely. One extreme would be to cross that line which we discussed earlier between frugality and cheapness.

Hoarding: Another subset of frugality is hoarding. Most of us, even spendthrifts, will not throw something away if we think there is a good chance we will need it in the future. A hoarder may not buy any more or less than the average person, but he can't throw anything away. He carries hoarding to such an extreme that it interferes with his everyday living. Hoarders typically retained so many items that they have difficulty finding something when they really need it. That's the first sign that one is a hoarder.

So how much retention constitutes hoarding? That is often a function of the number of items, size of the items, the space available, and the degree to which the hoarder is organized.

A person who lives in a rural area, has a four-car garage, and is organized, can "retain" far more, and still not be a hoarder, than the person who lives in a one bedroom apartment in Chicago.

Similarly, more and more people are becoming "electronic hoarders," saving so many pictures, music, or other digital files on their computers that they can't find anything that they are looking for. Again, the degree such hoarding is dysfunctional is primarily a function of organization or lack thereof.

The Pain Of Paying: For frugal people, the "joy of saving" in anticipation of future consumption is somewhat nebulous, hard to define, largely because the saver often is uncertain of what the future consumption may involve. It may be a long-planned vacation, a child's college education, keeping the home out of foreclosure, an early retirement, or taking advantage of some unknown opportunity, or even none of the above.

The frugal person is often motivated not so much by the "joy of saving", but by the "pain of paying." Thus, spending decisions often involve a tradeoff between the "pleasure of consumption" versus the "pain of paying." For the spendthrift, the pain of paying is negligible, whereas for the frugal person, such pain is many times greater.

Emotional Rewards: Frugality comes with its own set of emotional rewards just like consumerism. Frugal persons take pride in their ability to avoid the social pressure to spend, pride in their ability to resist temptations offered by pervasive advertising that each of us are exposed to every day. They take joy with the satisfaction with what they do have and do enjoy. Frugal persons often derive greater pleasure out of not spending than in finding a great deal. Frugal persons are often "sales pressure adverse," reacting very negatively to pressure to buy immediately. The greater the sales pressure, the more likely the frugal person won't buy.

The frugal person is more likely to buy a coat that is advertised as "60% off" than if advertised "60% off, but only if you buy today." The frugal person thinks, "The store wants me to buy immediately so I won't have a chance to reconsider the wisdom of this purchase."

Frugality begins with a commitment to self-control, self-sufficiency, independent thinking, and avoidance of debt. It's an acknowledgment that one cannot spend one's way to happiness, and that the important thing in life is not what you own but who you are.

Self-Control: Interestingly, the essential elements of frugality, such as self-control, independent thinking, and discipline are also important elements in leading a successful life.

Frugal people not only resist temptation ("I will not buy that winter coat that is priced 60% off because the coat I already have is sufficient"), but also actively reduce the occurrence of such temptations ("I will not go to the mall because there is nothing I desperately need.")

The Old Fashioned Way: In spite of all the publicity about people who fall into sudden wealth, such as entertainers, professional athletes, and lottery winners, most people with a moderate amount of wealth (say $500,000 to $5 million) got there the old fashion way: by being frugal, saving rather than spending, investing in themselves, in the stock market, in their own businesses, or in real estate.

Each person must choose his or her own road, but often these roads begin with having sufficient funds and minimal debts so as to take advantage of such opportunities. And as a recent graduate, that is where you are today (except for perhaps school loans).

In the next chapter we will explore how a small difference in spending habits can, over time, make a major difference in your wealth.

***

How a Small Difference in Spending Habits can make a Big Difference in your Net Worth.

"That man is the richest whose pleasures are the cheapest."
- Henry David Thoreau

Thrift: The art of obtaining wealth lies very much in thrift. All men are not equally qualified in earning money, but it is in everybody power to practice thrift. Consider carefully every expense. Is it really necessary? Can you buy the same product or service for less? If you do without the expense, will it matter a week, a month, or a year from now?

People frequently find that what they purchased yesterday is really not needed today. Yet, those same people too often fail to recognize that which they plan to purchase today, will not be what they need tomorrow. More often than not, items not purchased today usually are not missed tomorrow.

Limited Resources: We all have a limited amount of money to spend. We must spend it wisely, or else we go without those things that are more important to us. Pennies saved today, properly invested, can result in dollars tomorrow.

Beware of little expenses; coffee a little more costly; clothes a little finer; a little more entertainment. Is the pride of fine appearance worth the cost?

Pride cannot promote health nor ease pain; it makes no increase in the efficiency of a person; it creates envy; it hastens misfortune.

Buy what you have no great need for today, and before long you will have to sell your necessities! When the well is dry, we learn the worth of water. And so it is with money. Even the riches of the New World did not make Spain a rich nation because Spain's expenditures exceeded her income.

Methodology: In order to analyze the difference savings, income, and rates of return can make in wealth accumulation, we need to look at examples that compare two people and assume all else is the same, except for the variable we wish to examine.

This is commonly referred to as the "scientific method of testing", but it works for analyzing various aspects of wealth accumulation as well.

But, you may say, all other factors are never the same in real life. While that may be true, by isolating a specific expense, income earned, or investment rate earned, we can quantify the difference. Let's look at a few examples.

A Comparison: Allen and William both earn $40,000 per year after taxes. Allen is very frugal, buys reliable used cars and drives them for 10 to 12 years. William buys a new car every few years. Allen buys most of his clothes at Walmart, while William buys most of his at a major department store. Allen usually carries his lunch to work, while William typically goes out to restaurants for lunch.

Because of his frugality, Allen spends only $37,000 per year, thus saving $3,000, while William spends $43,000 per year, thus increasing his debt by $3,000 per year.

Allen invests his savings in a rental house and the stock market, and earns 10% per year. We will show you how such returns are quite possible in a later chapter. William "finances" his debt with credit cards, increasing his outstanding balance each year. Although William's credit cards started out at 0% interest, because he missed a couple of payments, his interest rate is now 21%.

Where do they stand financially after 20 years? Remember their differences in spending were only $6,000 per year. Well, Allen's savings ($3,000 per year) have grown to over $189,000. William, on the other hand, who has financed his $3,000 deficit per year, plus any finance charges, on his credit card, is $765,000 in debt! That is a difference of over $954,000 - simply because of a difference in spending of only $6,000 per year (or only about $16 per day.)

Interestingly, if Allen's twin brother had saved only $2,000 per year, and invested that $2,000 at only 5%, his brother would have accumulated only $69,438 in 20 years, but his net worth would still be over $830,000 more than William's net worth!

Hate Math? "I don't understand math! I hate it!" is a common complaint, and I understand why. Math often involves many complicated equations and calculations that either don't make sense or you would never use. The math of wealth creation, however, is relatively simple, and we will walk you through the simple math needed to make these calculations in a later chapter. So bear with me!

An Expensive Purchase: Richard and Thomas both earn the same amount, and spend exactly all of their earnings over a twenty year period, with only one exception. Thomas purchased a $2,000 TV at the beginning of the period on his credit card. Otherwise, ignoring interest charges, they have the same spending habits.

The compound interest on his credit card over 20 years at 21% interest would result in an outstanding balance of $90,518!

Actually, the interest charged may be considerably more, because not only did he pay interest on this purchase, but also on all of his other purchases, even though he paid off those other expenses each month, leaving just the TV and its finance charges on the credit card. Allen, on the other hand, paid off his balances each month, and never incurred any finance charges on any of his purchases.

Other Examples: Here's an example of how a small amount of increased income can make a difference. John and Frank each generally earn and save the same amount, except that John has a part time job in the winter and spring preparing tax returns, and in the summer painting houses.

As a result, John earns an extra $4,000 per year. Also, because he is working in his "spare time", he also spends $1,000 less than Frank. Like Allen in the earlier example, John invests that extra $5,000 per year at 10% for 20 years. That extra income/savings will grow to $315,000 over 20 years!

In another example let's assume that Ivan earns only $1,000 more than Charles and spends $1,000 less than Charles. Both are credit card debt free, both otherwise save a small amount each year. Ivan invests his extra $2,000 each year at 12%. At the end of 20 years, Ivan will have accumulated over $160,000 more than Charles.

To emphasize the difference in rate of return, let's assume that both invested $2,000 per year, but Ivan invests in real estate and earns 12% while Charles invests in CD's averaging 3%. At the end of 20 years, Ivan would have $106,000 more than Charles!

The Key To Wealth Accumulation: So the key to wealth accumulation for most recent graduates, immigrants, and newlyweds, is not sudden wealth of an inheritance, lottery, or the like, but is the gradual increase in their net worth over time through:

1. Minimizing expenditures
2. Increasing income
3. Increasing the return earned on the difference

Perhaps that is not what you wanted to hear, but that's it. That's how most people in this country accumulated their wealth. That's how the Vietnamese immigrant who could barely speak English and who came to this country with his family in 1975 with nothing, and managed to accumulate a net worth of over $4,000,000!

Before discussing how to minimize expenses, let's discuss the consequences of abusing credit cards and other forms of debt, as excessive debt is one the major impediments to the accumulation of wealth in America. In the next chapter, we will discuss how banks and credit card issuers can literally enslave you.

***

Slavery is NOT dead in America!

"We have met the enemy and they are us."
- Pogo

Voluntary Slavery: Your bank is your new master. But to a great extent, this slavery is voluntary. What do I mean by this?

I define slavery to mean conditions under which all or a significant part of your work efforts are required to be turned over to another. The person who earns $2,000 per month and is paying $500 per month on his credit card debt (of, say, $25,000 at 2% per month) is enslaved by his credit card company, usually a bank.

High Interest Rates: Perhaps you are asking, "Why would anyone pay 24% (2% per month) for credit card debt when so many credit cards seem to be offered with 0% interest?" Michael can answer that question.

"Well, it all started out with 0%. My wife and I had several credit cards with 0% interest, but we probably spent more than we should have. We paid only the minimum required. Why pay more with zero interest? But in the second year my wife had a large dental bill and we missed several payments. Our credit card companies increased our interest rate to 15% and, within a few months, increased the interest rate to 24%."

"We applied for a new card with a low interest, but we were declined because our existing credit card company had already reported our missed payments to all the major credit rating agencies."

Soon our other credit cards companies increased their rates as well because of our lower credit rating. One card even raised its rate to 29.99%. I guess they didn't have the guts to call it 30%!"

"In retrospect, we probably would have been better off if we had been late on only one or two cards, but we felt that since we couldn't afford to make all of our payments, we didn't make any. That was probably stupid."

"So there we were: Suddenly with large credit card debt, 24% interest rate and no reasonable way to get out. With the higher rates, we could barely make the much higher minimum payments."

"We did consider filing for a "Chapter 7 Bankruptcy", but our attorney told us that much of our debt was non-dischargeable, meaning that we would not be relieved of liability for such debt. So we were trapped!"

Getting Out Of Debt: What can they do? In a later chapter we will discuss getting out of debt. We will discuss some ways to reduce the effective interest rate you are paying and pay off the debt sooner. With close attention to debt management and self-discipline, most people can eliminate this form of enslavement in just a few years.

With continued discipline and following some of the advice in this book, most people can achieve a comfortable level of wealth in the following decade.

Read The Fine Print: Another common interest rate trap is "Buy now and make no payments until January!" True, no payments are required, but often interest is compounded at 21% or more per annum from the date of purchase!

"Zero interest for eighteen months" is another familiar marketing ploy, often to get you to buy things you don't really need at prices you can't afford! Read these contracts carefully, for what the large print gives, the small print takes away.

The fine print often advises you that if you do not pay in full by the end of the eighteen months, interest is charged from the date of purchase, often at over 20%! They don't even remind you of this at the end of the period, because they hope you won't fully repay to balance.

Not Deductible: Credit card debt is one of the worst forms of debt a person can have. Unlike home mortgage interest, credit card interest is not deductible. The rate is often 24% or more per annum.

2% per month (24% per year) may not sound like much. Gee, on a $2,000 television, that's only $40 per month. But if you are constantly in debt to credit card companies over 10 years, that $2,000 television will end up costing you over $4,800 in interest, and even more if the interest is not paid each month.

Payday Loans: But even worse are short-term unsecured loans, such as payday loans. A payday loan lender might loan you $400 on the 15th of the month to be repaid at the end of the month for "only a $40 service charge." It doesn't sound like much to someone who wants to buy an expensive television before the Super Bowl; why wait until the end of the month?

Note, however, that the borrower is paying 10% ($40) for the use of $400 for only fifteen days. That's an effective interest rate of over 250% per annum. If you obtain five such loans per year, you will pay $200 annually.

What if you had used that $200 per year to pay off existing credit card debt? If you otherwise carry credit card debt at 24%, $200 per year over 20 years would have saved you over $75,000!

In other words, if instead of getting the payday loan you had used the interest you would have paid on the payday loan to pay toward your credit card balance, you would be $75,000 less in debt after 20 years. If the payday loan is not paid on time, with late fees the effective interest rate could be much greater!

Gotcha! Credit is a clever financial trick that enables us to spend what we don't have. Credit cards are great for convenience, but are a terrible method of borrowing money. To accumulate wealth, acquire things the old fashion way: Save for them and pay cash, or at least pay the credit card balance in full each month.

The Good Credit Cards: Nevertheless, you almost need a credit card to survive these days. It's almost impossible to rent an automobile without a credit card. Paying for gasoline with cash takes twice as long as paying at the pump with a credit card. Moreover, many cards are available with no annual fee and no interest if, and this is a big if, if you pay off the outstanding balance during the grace period (typically 25 days following the billing date.)

Many credit cards also offer a rebate, some in cash, and some in frequent flyer miles. A typical rebate may be 1% or more on all of your purchases. Use such a card for those things that you would purchase anyway. If you charge $5,000 per year, that's an extra $50 in your pocket!

Some cards even offer a 3% to 5% rebate on selected categories and a 1% on everything else. But whatever credit card you select, watch for changes in the terms. Banks will frequently change both the bonus rates as well as the categories to which the rebates apply.

Beware Of Overdraft Charges: Debit cards offer another alternative to the traditional credit card. A debit card is almost like writing a check in that the funds "charged" are deducted from your checking account at the time of purchase. Just be careful to avoid any overdraft charges!

George charged six items one day, all under $10 and totaled less than $40. He didn't have sufficient funds in his account, as his payroll check was two days late in being credited to his account. The bank honored each charge, but then charged him $33 for each overdraft, for a total of $198! When his payroll check was finally credited to his account, the bank withdrew most of it to cover these overdraft charges, which in turn triggered another round of overdrafts.

It's Your Choice: Yet, many people who properly manage their credit never have an annual fee, never have a finance charge, and earn a rebate each year.

So, the choice is yours. To stop the slavery, you must stop the spending. The road to wealth begins by ending the slavery and starting the accumulation phase of your life. A journey of a thousand miles begins with a single step. Control your expenditures. Buy only that which is really needed and needed now.

And this leads us to our next chapter, titled "Minimizing Expenditures."

***

Minimizing Expenditures

*"Many a man loses far more money through the hole
at the top of his pocket than the hole at the bottom."*

Expenditures vs. Expenses: This chapter is titled minimizing EXPENDITURES rather than EXPENSES because many people have a limited view of what their expenses are. Is purchasing that antique couch an expense or an investment? Many people do not think of many of their larger purchases as expenses, but they will acknowledge that such purchases are expenditures. Thus, this chapter is about minimizing all expenditures, not just "expenses."

An expenditure is any exchanging of money for something which is not an appropriate investment. When we refer to "saved" or "savings" in this book, we refer to money not spent, money that you still have to invest or spend later. Savings is the opposite of expenditures.

Spending Habits: The greatest impediments to achieving wealth in America for most people are their spending habits. The average adult is bombarded with an average of over 500 advertising messages per day to buy, buy, buy. Even the advertisements that mention the word "save" have nothing to do with reducing expenditures, such as in "Save 20% if you buy today!" That is not exactly what we mean by saving, although if you really needed the product and were going to buy it anyway, then there is certainly an advantage to paying less.

The Eyes Of Others: "Look at all those ads! It's our eyes that keep us in poverty!" my friend Fred stated. "No," his wife replied,

"It's not your eyes that keep us poor. All parts of our body require some expense. Our feet demand shoes; our body, clothing; our belly, food. Even our eyes require relatively cheap spectacles as we age. It is the eyes of other people that keep us in poverty. If all but us were blind, we should want neither fine clothes nor fine furniture. One reason why birds and horses are not unhappy is because they are not trying to impress other birds and horses."

Basic human needs are actually easily obtained in America today; human wants, by comparison, know no boundaries and thus are infinite. As one advertising executive stated, "Yes, I understand that nobody even wants this product today, but with enough advertising and exposure, people will not only want it, but consider it a basic human need."

Necessities Evolve Over Time: There's much truth in that statement. Think back to the early 1950's. A 12 inch black and white television gradually became something that everybody not only wanted, but actually needed. By the 1960's, a 19 inch color TV had replaced the black and white set as a necessity. Today, a 65 inch HD smart television is viewed by many as a necessity.

Similarly, a computer became (almost) a necessity by the late 1990's. Nevertheless, don't fall into the trap of thinking that something is a necessity, when in reality, it is a luxury that your future cannot afford.

People who bought the computer in the early 1990's found that they needed to buy another one by the late 1990's. People who waited not only saved the two thousand dollars that a basic computer cost back then, but now have the earnings on that $2,000 invested during the past seven years. Furthermore, they were able to buy a far better computer in 1999 for half of what they spent in 1992.

Also, buy the lowest price item that will meet your needs. Experience has shown that buying a computer which cost twice as much as what you really need does not extend its life by anywhere near that much.

Major And Minor Expenditures: Take as much care regarding small expenses as large expenses. A small leak can sink a great ship. Trusting too much to the care of others has been the ruin of many. "For want of a nail, the horseshoe was lost; for want of a horseshoe, the horse was lost; for want of a horse, the rider was lost; for want of a rider, the war was lost, all for the want of a horseshoe nail!"

Reduced Expenditures Result In Wealth! To reduce expenditures, you should consider all alternatives to spending less on necessities, and not buying anything else at all, or at least postponing the purchase until you can pay cash. Even small expenditures can be reduced. Saving (not spending) $5 per day doesn't sound like much, but it does amount to $1,825 per year. That's $18,250 over ten years without interest, and $36,500 over twenty years. Moreover, if that $5 per day can be invested each year at only 5%, over 20 years it would grow to $63,362; invested at 10%, it would grow to almost $115,000! And that is saving only $5 per day!

On the other hand, if spending that $5 results in your carrying credit card balances over the 20 year period at 24%, the true cost of wasting that $5 per day over twenty years is over $687,000.

Quit Smoking: Let's discuss several ways you can save $5 per day. For those who smoke even less than one pack of cigarettes a day, just quitting smoking can save literally a small fortune just in the cost of the cigarettes. And that doesn't take into consideration the additional potential savings on health costs, clothing damage, and the like.

Drink Water: When dining out, order tap water instead of a soft drink. That will save you perhaps $3.00 (after tax and tip) per meal. The savings will be even greater when you order water instead of a beer or glass of wine, where the savings may be $7.00 or more.

That may not sound like much, but if you and your companion dine out twice a week, the savings by not buying the soft drinks amounts to over $600 per year, or over $3,000 over 5 years. The savings by not buying the beer or glass of wine may amount to over $1,400 per year, or over $7,000 over 5 years. Not only will you save money, but water is generally healthier for you.

Lunch: Joe goes out every workday for a $7.00 lunch (with tax and tip.) Bill packs his lunch and eats it every day at his desk, spending only $2 or less. Not only does Bill get more work done, but he also saves $5 per day on lunch.

Parking: Joe parks in the lot next to the downtown office at $12 per day. Bill parks two blocks away and pays only $7. Not only does Bill get more exercise, but he also saves $5 per day.

The difference in the lunch and parking habits means that, other things being equal, Bill will save $10 per workday, or $2,500 per year. Invested at 10%, that $10 per day means Bill's net worth will be over $157,000 greater than Joe's net worth in 20 years. The difference would be even greater if Joe carries credit card balances at high interest rates to finance his other expenditures.

Clothes: Joe buys his suits at a department store for $350; Bill pays $100 for his suit (including tailoring) at a used suit store. Joe pays $55 for his shirts, $0 for his ties. Bill buys all of his shirts at Target on sale for $10, and ties for $10 each.

If both men buy one suit, four shirts, and four ties each year, Bill will spend $550 less than Joe each year on clothes. Over thirty years that savings each year invested at only 5% will grow to $38,368; at 10% to $99,518. At an earnings rate of 15%, it would grow to almost $275,000.

Automobiles: Joe buys a new car every other year, and a relatively expensive one, for $35,000. Bill buys used cars, typically a two or three year old Honda for $15,000 every five years. Over time, Bill will spend an estimated $5,000 less each year than Joe on automobile acquisition costs after trade-ins.

The difference in sales tax, annual registration, and insurance adds another $1,000 per year. Joe's car gets 20 miles per gallon, while Bill's car gets 25 miles per gallon. Both drive 10,000 miles per year; at $3.00 per gallon, that's another $300 per year that Bill saves.

Some readers will point out that Bill with his older cars is likely to have greater maintenance and repair expenses. And certainly most cars as they age do have more repairs than others. So, let's assume that Bill has $300 greater maintenance each year; that offsets the mileage advantage. Thus, Bill spends $6,000 less each year on an automobile than Joe.

If Bill invested that difference at only 5% for 20 years, that investment would grow to $208,315; at 10% it would grow to $378,000. Invested at 10% over 30 years, the savings would grow to over $1,085,000!

Conclusion: The less you pay for your car, the better the mileage, and especially, the longer you keep your cars, the more wealth you are likely to accumulate.

Buying low-cost, well-built cars, and keeping them for 10 years, rather than buying a new car every other year, may result in a $1 million greater net worth over a 30 year period!

Now That's An Expensive TV! We saw earlier how a onetime expenditure for an expensive television for $2,000 if financed on credit cards over a long period of time can end up costing a small fortune. Albert and Robert both earned and spent the same amount of money over the first twenty-five years of their lives. But Albert bought things before he could pay for them by using his credit card; Robert bought them later for cash (or paid off his credit card balance each month).

That is to say, Albert was always living on the next month's paycheck, whereas, Robert was always living on last month's paycheck. If Albert carried that $2,000 television purchase on a credit card balance at 24% for only ten years, it would ultimately cost him over $17,000!

Benjamin Franklin once said that a penny saved is a penny earned. He was wrong. A penny saved and invested at 12% over 30 years would actually grow to 30 cents! That doesn't sound like much, until you realize that $1,000 saves grows to $30,000, and that $10,000 saved (like in putting off buying that new car) grows to $300,000!

Haircuts: After he was married, John's wife suggested that he use her hair salon every other week to get his hair cut, paying $50 for a haircut. Later, he decided to go back to getting a similar hair cut once a month at Cost Cutters for $15. That was a savings of $85 per month on haircuts, or $1,000 per year. Saving $1,000 per year amounts to $20,000 over twenty years. Invested at 5%, that savings will grow to $34,719 over 20 years; at 10% it will grow to more than $63,000 over 20 years; and to more than $180,000 over 30 years!

Other Savings: Let's look at other ways you can save money and still not compromise the value of your purchase. Generic drugs (prescription and over the counter) and generic cosmetic products offer significant savings. Buying non-perishable goods in bulk usually offers considerable savings, especially if you won't use more of the product simply because you have more in the house. For example, aspirin and toilet paper fall into this category; potato chips do not. Aspirin is aspirin. Buy the least expensive brand you can find.

Although it is usually cheaper to eat at home than to eat even at fast food establishments, considerable savings are possible by selective shopping. For instance, George and Mary discovered that eating at McDonald's with their three children typically cost about $6.00 more than eating at Taco Bell. McDonald's Happy Meal undoubtedly made Ray Kroc (the founder of McDonald's) very happy!

Similarly, by ordering off the $1 menu you often get just as much food and sometimes for half the price. Again, let's run the numbers. Assume you eat at fast food places twice a week, and can save $6 each time. You would save $12 per week, or over $600 per year. Invested at only 5% for 20 years, that $600 per year will grow to over $20,000. If that same savings were invested at 10%, it would grow to over $37,800.

From Hundreds To Millions! Hopefully, this chapter has demonstrated how wasting a couple of hundred dollars a month can make the difference between being broke and being a millionaire in 30 years!

Don't buy expensive wine, luggage, or watches. Few people can tell the difference from a $50 bottle of wine and "Two Buck Chuck."

Expensive luggage dramatically increases the chance that your luggage will be stolen, as any thief would assume there are expensive things inside. I saw a $12,000 Rolex in the jewelry store window, and, believe it or not, it had the exact same time as the ten dollar Timex on my wrist.

I once noticed a wealthy neighbor on a ladder cleaning out his gutters. I asked him, "Can't you afford to hire someone to do that?" To which he replied, "In order to pay someone $200 to do this, I would have to earn $400, and for $400, I will do it myself!" Perhaps that statement summarizes why he is wealthy!

Play By The Rules: Several rules may help you reduce your expenditures:

1. If you can't pay cash, don't buy it.
2. If you don't really need it, don't buy it.
3. If you think you do really need it, wait until tomorrow.
4. Buy well-built cars and keep them for over ten years.
5. Save by buying non-perishable items in bulk or on a super sale.
6. Avoid expensive stores and restaurants.
7. Live as economically the day after payday as you did the day before!
8. If you go shopping at the mall, as you walk around, make a list of all the things you are considering buying. But don't buy them then. Go home. Then go back to the mall two days later and buy only those things you still think you really need. The average person will concede that over half of the items on the list really aren't needed.

Beware Of Large Signs: Don't be tricked by a "large sign" in the middle of the shopping aisle. What do I mean by that?

One of the major "Marts" did a survey several years ago. They placed an item in the middle of the shopping aisle as you walk into the store. The item was priced at $4.79. A week later they priced the item at only $4.29 - a fifty-cent reduction - with a larger sign. Daily sales of the item increased by 20%. They concluded that the lower price increased sales.

Then someone questioned whether it was the lower price or larger sign. So the next week they increased the price to $5.29 (fifty cents more than the original price) and doubled the size of the sign. Much to everybody's surprise, sales of the item further increased by 12%.

The Moral: A large price sign don't necessarily mean that the item is a good buy. As with everything else, you can't believe what you read on signs, hear on the radio, or see on television!

Beware Of Sales: Never buy something you don't need just because it is on sale. Never buy what you do not really need because the price is cheap. Store sales can be seductive. Know what is a good price for the things you plan to buy. And, remember, a large sign does not necessarily mean a good value.

Saving 40% off on an item you do not need is really wasting 60%! Remember that a good price is not necessarily the price at which the item is offered, but what the item is worth to you.

Frugality Revisited: A friend of mine once ridiculed my frugality by saying, "Gee, you save a dime here and a dime there, and before you know it, you have 20 cents!" inferring that it wasn't worth the effort. I later calculated that if I saved 20 cents per day, and invested it at 15%, such savings would grow to over $36,000 over 30 years.

I would rather have people laugh at my cheapness than for me to weep later at my extravagances. That man is richest whose pleasures are the cheapest, for he who buys what he does not need will soon need what he cannot buy. For when your outgo exceeds your income, your upkeep will be your downfall.

He who can live on little, compared to his salary, is likely to be more content and less subject to dishonest actions, than he who earns more, but spends even more. It's funny how some people think of frugal people as being less virtuous. Frugality and the accumulation of wealth generally have little to do with the lack of virtue.

Even The IRS Knows This: Actually, it is the man in want who spends more than he earns, who finds it more difficult to act honestly. That is why when the I.R.S. looks for undeclared income; it looks first to the spending habits of the taxpayer. It is a proven fact that those who spend more than they appear to earn are the ones most likely to be under reporting income.

The biggest crooks in the world have traditionally been those who try to impress others with their wealth. I would sooner trust a man in old blue jeans than a man in expensive clothes wearing a lot of gold jewelry. A man who spends more than he makes is the one more likely to "borrow" from his friends or clients, even though he has no reasonable means of repaying the money. Jails are full of big spenders who claimed they always intended to repay the money that they had wrongfully taken from others.

It is not the frugal man who is less trustworthy, but is the person who spends more than he makes. The moral here, of course, is to be very leery of flashy people who want you to invest your money with them. Their last investor probably paid for that expensive car they are driving.

That Second Million: It has long been observed that it is considerably easier to accumulate the second million dollars than it was to accumulate the first million. A common observation by retirees is that they will make more on their investments next year by "doing nothing" than they saved during their first ten years of their working career. Of course, without those first ten years of savings, they would not have accumulated much of which they are investing today.

We have mentioned a lot of numbers so far. Are they accurate? Where do they come from? How do we know that 20 cents per day invested at 15% will grow to over $36,000 in 30 years?

We will examine how these numbers are developed in the next chapter.

***

The Mathematics of Wealth Creation

Chevy Chase, posing as a presidential candidate on Saturday Night Live, was asked by a reporter: "Last year the economy grew at 2.6% while unemployment decreased to 5.1%, and the trade deficit grew by $1.24 billion. How would your proposed economic policy affect these figures?" To which Chevy replied, "I was told there wouldn't be any math on this exam."

"The most amazing thing in the universe is compound interest!"
- Albert Einstein

Somewhere between comic genius and true genius lies the truth.

Math And Motivation: Understandably, many people have trouble with math and simply wish to avoid it. Yet understanding at least some of the concepts of wealth accumulation is important, if for no other reason than it may provide the motivation you need to spend less, save more, earn more, and invest for greater returns.

When a successful businessman was asked why he was so successful, he commented: "We make them for $2.00 each and sell them for $4.00 each, and it's amazing how that 2% profit adds up!" Of course, he was joking, as a profit of $2.00 on an item that sells for $4.00 is not a 2%, but 50% on the selling price, or 100% of the cost of producing the item.

To understand the mathematics of compound interest, you need only use simple math: Multiplication and Addition.

Percentages: A percentage is merely one number divided by another number, and then multiplied by100. Alternatively, think of it as the division with the decimal point moved to the right two places.

For example: $10 is what percent of $100? The answer: 10/100=.1, or 10%. Conversely, 10% of 100 equals 10.

Simple Interest: With simple interest the interest rate is applied to the beginning balance. For example, if you invest $100 for 5 years at 10% simple interest, the interest would be .1 (which is 10%) times $100 times 5 (years), which equals $50.

At the end of the period of time you would have principal (your original investment of $100) plus the interest ($50) for a total of $150.

Compound Interest: With compound interest, the interest rate is applied to the new balance each period, which would include the prior period's interest.

Let's see how 10%, compounded annually, would work. We have created a chart on the following page below to demonstrate this principle.

The beginning balance (Column B) times the interest rate (Column C) yields the interest earned (Column D) for the period, which when added to the beginning balance (Column B) gives us the ending balance (Column E), which in turn then becomes the beginning balance (Column B) for the next year:

A	B	C	D	E
	Beginning	Interest	Interest	Ending
Year	Balance	Rate	Earned	Balance
1	$100.00	10%	$10.00	$110.00

The ending balance of year 1 is the beginning balance of year 2:

| 2 | $110.00 | 10% | $11.00 | $121.00 |

The ending balance of year 2 is the beginning balance of year 3:

| 3 | $121.00 | 10% | $12.10 | $133.10 |

The ending balance of year 3 is the beginning balance of year 4:

| 4 | $133.10 | 10% | $13.31 | 146.41 |

The ending balance of year 4 is the beginning balance of year 5:

| 5 | $146.41 | 10% | $14.64 | 161.05 |

Thus, if you invest $100 at 10% compound interest, at the end of five years the value of your investment would be $161.05.

Compound Interest vs. Simple Interest: Compare the ending values with compound interest to simple interest. With compound interest our initial investment of $100 grew to $161.05, rather than $150 with simple interest. The difference may not seem great in this example, but the higher the interest rate and the longer the period of time, the more dramatic the difference.

Another way to compare compound interest to simple interest is to think of simple interest as what the investment would grow to if you spent the interest each year and of compound interest as what the investment would grow to if you left the interest each year in the account of investment.

Compound Interest Tables: By using a computer spreadsheet, such as Microsoft Excel, we can generate a table showing the ending values for various rates and periods for, say, an initial investment of $100. Thus, the reader doesn't have to do these basic calculations. We have included such a table near the end of this book as Appendix A.

Rather than having a massive table that gives the value of every year, we have decided to abbreviate the table and show only the accumulated value in five year periods. For the purposes of this book, this table will be sufficient to demonstrate the principals of wealth accumulation. We have and will use this table throughout this book when discussing how wealth is accumulated. Knowing the exact numbers is not as important as appreciating the concepts.

The reader can now uses the table in Appendix A to determine the ending value of $100 invested at a given percent, for a given number of years, and then multiply that value times the number of "hundreds" in the initial investment for which you are calculating the future value.

Simple interest at 10% For 30 Years: With simple interest, we know that $100 invested for 30 years at 10% interest would earn interest of $300 (10% times $100 times 30 years), and thus we would have the interest plus the beginning balance at the end of the thirty year period for a total of $400.

Using The Appendix A Table: In order to calculate how much we would have at the end of 30 years with the interest compounded, we refer to Appendix A. Look up the factor for 30 years at 10%. With compound interest (refer to the table in Appendix A) that same $100 invested at 10% for 30 years would have grown to $1,744.94, or more than 4 times as much as in the simple interest example!

If the initial investment were more or less than $100, we would merely multiply the factor in the table times the number of "hundreds" in our initial investment. Thus, an initial investment of $2,500 would have grown to $43,623.50 (2500/100=25; 25 times $1,744.94 equals $43,623.50).

Compound interest is a double-edged sword, as this concept also works in reverse for money borrowed for a given number of years. Thus, if Joe borrows $2,000 (remember our expensive television example?) on his credit card that charges a 24% annual interest rate.

If the credit card company allowed him to keep that balance and plus the finance charges on his credit card for 10 years, the ultimate cost of that television, including the initial cost and interest on the credit card, would total $17,188.80! Over thirty years, the balance would grow to over $1,269,000.

Let's examine how that amount is calculated. We look at the table in Appendix A across the top to find the column labeled 10 years. Next, we go down that column until we see 24% on the left side of the table. The "factor" would be $859.44.

Remember, the table in Appendix A is for an initial investment (or debt in this example) of $100. Divide $2,000 (the initial loan) by $100, and that equals 20. Let's double check our math: It would take twenty $100 bills to make $2,000. Yes, that looks correct.

Viewed another way, you simply move the decimal place of the initial investment two places to the left (2000. becomes 20.00). Next, we multiply 20 times the factor shown in the table. Thus, 20 times 859.44 equals $17,188.80.

That's how much principal and interest this person would have paid had Joe (1) charged the TV on his credit card, and (2) carried a balance for ten years of at least $2,000 plus accrued interest on his credit card which charges 24% interest per year.

Other Examples: Viewed another way, let's assume that John, who always pays off his credit card balances, doesn't buy the TV, but instead invests that $2,000 in a rental house.

Let's further assume that the rental house earns an average of 15% per year for that same 10 years.

Note that I did not say appreciates at 15%. If he puts 10% down and the property appreciates at only 4% per year, that's a 40% return the first year on his investment! Because the equity grows, the return on each year's new equity tapers off after that first year. Assume for the sake of this example that the 15% return on investment is obtainable.

So how much wealth has John accumulated after 10 years? Go to Appendix A, look for 10 years across the top, and go down to the row labeled 15%. That intersection gives us a factor of $404.56. Remember that the table in Appendix A is per $100 of initial investment. Multiply the table factor by 20, as explained above, and the investment of $2,000 would have grown to $8,091.20.

Query: How much would the $2,000 initial investment have grown to over 30 years at 15%?

The Appendix A factor is $6,621.18, multi- plied by 20, equals $132,423.60. Notice that the longer the period and the higher the interest rate, the more dramatic the growth. That observation was the source of Einstein's quote above.

Another example: Jim saved the $25 given to him for his birthday by his aunt. Initial investment (savings) is $25. Move the decimal place 2 places to the left equals .25, which we then multiply times the applicable factor from the table.

If Jim invested that $25 at 10% for 15 years, the factor 417.72 would be multiplied by .25 which equals $104.43. Thus, $25 invested at 10% for 15 years would grow to $104.43.

Annual Investments: The table in Appendix A shows the future value of an initial investment of $100. But what if that same investment had been made every year? How do you calculate the future value investing $100 <u>per year</u>? This math, too, is relatively simple.

Let's go back to our original calculations for the table in Appendix A, and simply add the $100 initial investment to the beginning balance for each year after the first year, then calculate the interest on that new beginning balance:

A	B	C	D	E
	Beginning	Interest	Interest	Ending
Year	Balance	Rate	Earned	Balance
1	$100.00	10%	$10.00	$110.00

The ending balance of year 1 PLUS $100 is the new beginning balance of year 2, and so on for each year thereafter:

2	$210.00	10%	$21.00	$231.00
3	$331.00	10%	$33.10	$364.10
4	$464.10	10%	$46.41	$510.51
5	$610.51	10%	$61.05	$671.56

Thus, if you had invested $100 each year at 10% compound interest, the value of your investment after 5 years would be $671.56.

Once again, by using a computer spreadsheet, such as Microsoft Excel, we can generate a table (Appendix B at the end of this book) showing the ending values for various rates and periods. Thus, the reader doesn't have to do the basic calculations. As before, rather than having a massive table that gives the value of every year, we have decided to abbreviate the table in Appendix B and show only the accumulated value in five year periods.

Using The Appendix B Table: Let's look at an example. As we stated in Chapter 6, saving (not spending) $5 per day doesn't sound like much, but it does amount to $1,825 per year ($5 times 365). If that $5 per day can be invested at 10% over 20 years, the mere $5 per day will grow to $114,979!

Let's see how that future value is calculated. We look at the table in Appendix B across the top to find the column labeled 20 years. We go down that column until we see 10% on the left side of the table. The "factor" for $100 per year would be $6,300.25.

Remember, the table in The Table in Appendix B is for an <u>annual</u> investment of $100. Divide $1,825, the annual investment, by $100, and that yields 18.25.

Alternatively, simply move the decimal place of the annual investment two places to the left (1825 becomes 18.25). Multiply the factor shown in the table in Appendix B ($6,300.25) times 18.25 equals $114,979.

What if the $5 per day could have been invested at 15% over 30 years? How is that calculated? Referring to Appendix B the table shows a factor of $49,995.69 for 15% over 30 years. Multiplied by 18.25, the future value would be $912,421! Saving just saving $5 every day and investing it at 15% over 30 years will grow to almost one million dollars!

Savings Throughout The Year: The astute reader may point out that we really don't have the $1,825 at the beginning of the year to invest, but that the $1,825 was saved over a twelve month period. Yes, that is correct. On average, the $5 per day was really saved mid-year, not at the beginning of the year.

So whenever we have referred to a period of time with respect to accumulation of annual investments that are actually save continuously throughout the year, we would need to add approximately one-half of a year to the number of years.

Thus, the future value of investing the $5 per day at 10% for twenty years, which the table shows to be $114,979, would really be the value after twenty years and six months. We have rounded down in the sake of simplicity in our calculations and in our analysis in this book.

More complex tables could be developed for monthly, weekly, and even daily investments, but these two tables in the appendix are all we need to demonstrate the basic principles of wealth accumulation.

The Only Tables We Need: So now we have two tables. And, basically, that's all we need for most of our mathematical calculations. To summarize, we have developed two interest rate tables:

Appendix A for the future value of an Initial Investment of $100.00.

Appendix B for the future value of Annual Investments of $100.00.

Hopefully, it is becoming obvious that wealth is largely accumulated by not spending all of your income and then investing those savings at relatively high rates of return over time.

Financial Calculators: There are many financial calculators, such as the HP 12C that I have used for years, as well as electronic versions of such tools. These analytical tools often come with an extensive manual that is the equivalent of a college course in finance. Those wishing to further explore the financial analysis of investing and wealth accumulation are encouraged to obtain one or more of these tools.

Time: This chapter demonstrates not only the importance of earnings over time, but also the importance of time itself. It is time that magnifies earnings.

Time can also make us more proficient. Time used wisely can enhance our earnings, not only through compounding of returns, but also by increasing our ability to earn money. Time used to enhance your earning power can be just as powerful as time used for compounding returns.

Time also expands our ability to use money wisely. A dollar spent today is a dollar less available tomorrow, and even greater with earnings over a multi-year period. Many people poorly analyze the opportunities lost by impulsive shopping.

A few dollars wasted yesterday and today may mean that you won't have the money several years from now for the glamorous vacation, for your child's first year of college, or for the new car you may desperately need when your old one breaks down.

As one person put it, there is a huge difference between have an old car and no car at all. By comparison, the difference between a five year old car and a brand new one is relatively small.

Furthermore, just as budgeting your money is important, so is budgeting your time. It has often been said, "Time is Money!"

How you use your time can be a great help, or a great hindrance, to wealth accumulation.

Don't have enough time? Bill Gates, Jeff Bezos, and Mark Zuckerberg, perhaps three of the richest man in America, have the exact same amount of time each day as you and I have - 24 hours. It's what you do with those 24 hours that makes a difference.

Before we discuss how to maximize your income, we have three chapters on time management.

The next chapter is titled the "The $100,000 Idea" which emphasizes the first tool in our Time Management toolbox. Why is time management important in creating wealth? Just as we have a limited amount of financial resources, we also have a limited amount of time resources.

That is why many people feel the next chapter - "The $100,000 Idea" - is the most important chapter in this book.

***

The $100,000 Idea!

"Pale ink is better than the best memory."

This chapter is included to help the reader get more out of life, whether it is reducing expenses, maximizing income, creating wealth, or just spending more time with your friends and family.

Many who have reviewed a draft of this book prior to publication have told the author that this was the most important chapter. You decide for yourself.

The Management Consultant: Nearly a century ago, Stan Morrison was a nationally-known management consultant. He was the guest speaker at an executive luncheon attended by Henry Ford, the founder of Ford Motor Company. Ford had heard of Morrison, and after the luncheon asked him about his services. Stan outlined them briefly, ending with a statement, "With our services you'll know how to manage better."

"Hell," shouted Ford, "I'm not managing as well now as I know how. What we need at Ford is not more knowing, but more doing. Not more knowledge, but more action. If you could only show us how to do half the things we already know we ought to be doing, show us how to get things done, I will be glad to engage your services and at any price."

Morrison thought for a moment and responded: "I can give you a lesson in 10 minutes that will help you get more done tomorrow."

"OK" agreed Ford, "I have just about 10 minutes before I have to leave to get back to the office. What's your lesson?"

The File Card: Morrison handed a 3" x 5" file card to Ford and told him, "Before you start work each day, spend ten minutes writing on this card the ten things that you need most to get done today. Then number them in the order of their importance."

"Next," said Morrison, "put this card in your pocket, and start working on number one. Look at the list every hour during the day until you have finished number one. Then tackle number 2; then number 3. Do this all day.

Do not be frustrated if you've only finished a few of the items, or even if you haven't finished number 1. You have been working on the most important items; the rest can wait. If you can't finish your entire list with this method, you can't with any other method either. And without this method, you probably won't even be working on the most important tasks."

Morrison continued, "Before starting on your next day's list, transfer all of your unfinished items from the prior day to a new card and spend five minutes every day adding new items of the day's most urgent tasks and prioritize them. After you have tried this method, have your key employees try it. Test this system for as long as you like and then send me a check for what you think it's worth."

The Check: Three months later Morrison received a check for $100,000 along with a note saying, "This simple little method is the most practical lesson I have ever learned in all of my life. It motivated me to make a phone call that I had put off six months. That phone call resulted in a $90 million order for Ford trucks."

A year later Morrison received another note from Henry Ford stating, "I later explained this simple procedure to my top executives. That did more to make Ford Motor Company the world's largest automobile company than all of the meetings I had held with these highly-paid executives."

Henry Ford learned like most great men learn that the simplest ideas often get the best results.

Sounds Too Simple? This simple little lesson is so plain sounding that the average person won't even try it. Because it is so simple, its results are almost unbelievable. But it has turned more floundering careers into high-achieving careers than any secret of success or any high-priced motivation course. Furthermore, it can be just as useful in your personal life as in your employment.

It beats all methods for turning ordinary people into extraordinary achievers. If you think that I am claiming too much for this humble little system, keep in mind that many highly successful people in business, in government, and even in teaching, have stated that this method is the most important factor in their success.

You will find successful people in all walks of life who use some adoption of this method. For getting things done it beats all the high-priced systems that have ever been invented.

Buy a couple of packs of 3" by 5" file cards today. Get started right away while these ideas are fresh in your mind. It only takes a few minutes, yet it might mark the turning point in your life as it has for so many other people.

Lower Your Initial Expectations: Don't expect your reaction the first day to be that this system is life-changing. If you are like most people when they first started to use this system, your reaction most likely will be, "Gee, I sure got a lot done today!"

If that is your reaction, keep using the system. It will be life-changing over time!

In seeking success, the hardest part is always the starting. A task begun is half done. Use one card every day for the rest of your life. It's not difficult, and you'll be surprised how quickly the habit will grow into an interesting game, the most profitable game that you'll ever play.

An Inexpensive Employee: You can hire an assistant to organize and motivate you for the price of a few packs of 3" x 5" file cards. File cards never forget. If you need to remember something, write it down. If you are constantly forgetting things, write them down. If you want to make the best use of your limited time on this earth, write it down.

I cannot over-emphasize the importance of writing things down on your file card. It can help you solve problems, accomplish difficult tasks, stop old bad habits, and develop new good ones. It can make you successful, even rich, if you will only write it down and study your file card each day.

Plant The Seed: Merely thinking about achieving something is time wasted. Listing the important things you want to achieve each day is like planting a seed in the ground. It grows, and over time, even a small acorn can become a great oak tree. Writing a thing down signals your subconscious mind to work on it, and that's what can turn your wish into reality.

Your daily list can be as long or as short as you wish. Your file card is like a ticket to greater achievement and success. You will use your time wisely. With your little file card, you will never be at a loss of what to do with a little extra time. Don't waste time; for that is the thing that life is made of. If it's worth remembering, if it's worth doing, it's worth writing down on your file card.

To further enhance your card system, make a habit of reading something inspiring and cheerful just before going to sleep. Keep a pen and paper on your night stand so if you get a great idea at three in the morning you can write it down.

Electronic Alternatives: Many people are now using their cell phones to create to do lists. Isn't this a step forward compared to the file card system? The answer is a definite "NO" - actually for three reasons:

1. It takes most people far longer to make any entry into their cell phone than to scribble the same thing on a piece of paper. (Example: "Pick up the dry cleaning on the way home".)

2. Deleting items accomplished in your cell phone does not provide the same emotional feeling of accomplishment as drawing a line through it on your file card.

3. The biggest objection to electronic reminder systems is the inability to see the big picture at a glance. Glancing at your file card allows you to see not only all of the remaining items to be accomplished today and their priorities, but also to see the items already accomplished.

Seeing what you have accomplished often provides the motivation to do more. Seeing the remaining items all at once allows you to better assign priorities so you are working on the most important items first. In these ways the file card system is still superior to most electronic reminder systems.

On the other hand, if you can achieve these objectives with your cell phone or other electronic device, more power to you. Try each method for a week or two to decide which one is most effective for you.

Additional Tools Needed: Those who use the "to do" list as their only "time management" tool have recognized that it tends to focus solely on the most urgent items. Often, very important items get neglected because they are not viewed as urgent in the day-to-day context.

The next two chapters, although brief, work together with your daily "to do" list. The first is on the use of calendars, and the second on goal setting. As you will see, these are necessary component of any time management system.

***

Use of Calendars

"So much time, so few days. What's a person to do?"

In addition to using the file card "to do" list system, and to enhance its productivity, it is important to use some form of a calendar system. Electronic calendars of upcoming events on a cell phone or on a computer can be useful, especially if the system permits the printing out of a full week or month in advance.

The Paper Calendar: Therefore, a paper calendar is recommended, even if used in conjunction with, or generated by, a computerized system. The paper calendar allows you to see all scheduled activities for the whole month at a glance.

For example, you may have an important project due in three weeks. Should it even be on your to-do list today? It helps to see how busy you are going to be during the next three weeks. Not only would the answer to that question help you decide if it goes on today's list, but also helps in assigning its priority.

For example, if you were extremely busy the next three weeks, but not so busy today, the project may not only go on list for today, but might be assigned a high priority. On the other hand, if you have already reserved the Monday before it's due to work on the project, it wouldn't even make today's to-do list. Glancing at a monthly calendar allows you to make these determinations far more easily than paging through each day's list in your cell phone.

Some people use their cell phone to log in action items each day. Then at the end of the day, they record them on their paper calendar at home, or even enter them into their computerized system from which they can periodically print out a paper calendar. One effective system has you begin each new action item entered into the cell phone with an asterisk ("*") and then delete the asterisk when the item is entered onto the paper calendar/computer system.

Use it With Your To-Do List: Each day when preparing your to-do list on the file card, it is important to consult your calendar, not only to determine which items to add, but to also assign priorities.

Those who have used the file card system have observed another major flaw. The card system tends to concentrate on accomplishing tasks that have the greatest urgency, and may neglect or omit tasks that may be more important in the long run, but seem less urgent today. A periodic review of your calendar helps you concentrate on both the urgent and the important, but only to the extent that such tasks are on your calendar. But what about your long term goals that don't appear on your calendar?

Long-Term Goals: For instance, you may have an important goal of buying a rental property. But that may never appear on your calendar, as it certainly doesn't have the urgency that requires that you work on that goal by a certain date. So how you can integrate important future goals with your calendar and to-do list is the topic of the next chapter.

***

Goal Setting

*Alice approached a Y in the road. "Which way ought I go
from here?" asked Alice. "That depends a good deal
on where you want to get to," replied the Cheshire Cat.
"But I don't care much where," said Alice.
"Then it doesn't matter which way you go," replied the Cat.*
– From "Alice in Wonderland" by Lewis Carroll.

Living your life without goals is like starting a journey without a map. What good is driving 100 miles only to later discover you drove in the wrong direction? Planning requires contemplation of the result, not just the process.

Stay On Track: Another reason for goal setting and measuring results is that you can get back on track early if you deviate. Imagine you are an Apollo astronaut racing to the moon. If you drift off course shortly after takeoff, the course adjustment is minor. An adjustment half way will require more energy. And if you wait until you are near the moon, you may not be able to make the necessary adjustment at all.

The biggest fear many Americans have is running out of money in their retirement. Yet very few Americans ever run the numbers to figure out what savings and rates of return are necessary to support their lifestyle. Most Americans spend more time planning their vacation than planning their retirement.

Most Americans spend more time watching TV in a week than they do in planning their future in a decade. Where do you want to be in ten years? Write it down. A man without goals is like a ship without a rudder. Create a list of your goals. What do you want to achieve, not only in terms of wealth, but also in terms of marriage, job satisfaction, children, where you want to live, and how your community will view you. What is important to you?

Goal Setting: Take control of your life. The greater danger for most of us is not setting our aim too high and falling short, but in setting our aim too low and achieving it.

Some people know exactly what their financial goals are. And maybe you do, too. Or maybe you're spending all your energy managing your current financial situation. If that's the case, it may take a special effort to concentrate on what you think is important for the future. But you'll find it's worth the time to consider where you want to be - what you would like to accomplish - in the next 5, 10, 20, even 30 years of your life. Visualize where you'd like to be when that time arrives.

There are some goals that most people share: staying out of debt, owning a home, starting a family, and having a secure retirement. Other goals may be more specific to who you are, such as paying for your children's college tuition or starting your own small business. What is important to you - or what may be important to you in the future?

What Are Yours? There are no right answers about what your goals should be. For some, merely planning for a financially secure future means that more specific goals can be more easily obtained later on. Beyond that, each person's plan is unique.

As part of the planning process, you'll want to ask yourself some important questions:

- Do you have enough cash saved in an emergency fund in case you lose your job or miss work because of an accident or illness?

- Do you want to go back to school? Is more education a key to a promotion at work? What is important for a new job or a new career?

- Will you need to support your parents after they retire?

- Are there other people who'll need your financial help?

- Do you hope to buy a home or upgrade to a larger one?

- Do you have children or plan to? Do you want them to go to college?

- At what age do you want to retire?

These questions are only starting points. You'll need to consider your unique needs, personal situation, and how much time you have to achieve your goals to determine the questions you need to ask and answer.

Life Is Full Of Changes: There may be events that you feel will make your planning more difficult or impossible. But don't be discouraged. Starting a family, buying a home, or even changing careers mid-life may affect your plans, but that is no reason not to plan.

Moreover, your situation may be different than the situation of your friends or family members. For example, if your youngest child will graduate from high school in the year you could take early retirement, your situation is different from someone who never had children or who had them very young. Your long-term goals and the timing for achieving them may be quite different than those of someone else.

One of the short comings of the file card systems described earlier is its possible failure of helping you to focus on very important things that are not currently urgent, and may never be urgent, but may be very important to your goals and the values in which you believe.

An Example: After reading this book, John realized the importance of buying a rental property. He also set a goal of spending more quality time with his children. A third goal was to try to visit his aging mother, who lives 300 miles away, at least four times each year.

As suggested in this chapter, John prepared a written list of these goals. He reviews them at least once per week. Reviewing these goals allows John to add items that are important to his file card and to his calendar.

In reviewing his calendar, John notices that his son has a soccer game next Saturday. Not only will John attend, but he also decides to take his family out for pizza afterward.

John puts a high priority on the soccer and the dinner, even though he would rather go with his friend Gary who has an extra ticket to the college football game that same Saturday. It was the review of his goals that convinced John that the soccer game was more important.

John notices on his calendar that nothing is scheduled for the following Saturday. He thought that maybe he would ask Gary over to watch the football game on television, but after reviewing his list of goals, John decides instead to call his real estate broker to set up showings of several rental properties for John to inspect on that Saturday.

It was only after reviewing his goals that he realized that looking at rental properties was more important in the long run than watching the game with Gary.

So John adds "Call real estate Broker" to his file card for today and assigns the call a high priority, even though the call is not urgent in the traditional sense, nor very time consuming. It has a high priority because it is important in John's long term goals. Without his list of goals, John might not have ever called the broker.

Lastly, John tentatively schedules all four visits to his mother on his calendar. Even though the dates aren't set in stone and can be rescheduled if necessary, John knows by having them on his calendar, those visits will not be forgotten.

Delaying a visit by a week or two won't upset his mother. John knows that the visits, although not urgent, are important, and are at least on his calendar.

What, No Goals? If you have no goals in life, it's later than you think, and you better get some. Without goals you might never achieve your potential. You may die without ever having been alive.

We have previously discussed how credit can enslave you. In the next chapter, and before discussing how to maximize your income, we will discuss what you really need to know about getting out of debt. If you are debt free, you may wish to skip this next chapter.

On the other hand if you are debt free and read it, it may scare you sufficiently to never get into debt in the first place!

***

The Real Secret to Getting out of Debt

"It has often been said that the toughest part of dieting is not watching what you eat; it's watching what your friends eat. And so it is with getting out of debt."

Background: The tough part is not appreciating that which you have as much as coveting that which your neighbor has. In fact, many people have borrowed so much just to "keep up with the Joneses" that their debt service has become a major expenditure. "Keeping up with the Joneses" is merely an expression meaning matching your neighbor's expenditures. It is often used as an acceptable method to justify buying something we would not otherwise purchase. It serves to protect us from the painful job of thinking for ourselves.

Several years ago there was an advertisement on television that featured George riding on his lawn-mowing tractor, talking about all the things he has, and then saying, "How do I do it? I'm in debt up to my eyeballs!" At least George was honest with himself! Of course, the easiest solution to this problem is to not get into debt to begin with!

The artificial wants of mankind have far exceeded the necessities. By these extravagances, many middle class Americans have been reduced to poverty, forced to borrow from those very banks they claim to despise. It is easier to suppress your first desire than to satisfy all that follow.

Success in life depends more on being satisfied with what you already have than on trying to acquire what you currently want.

Avoid Debt: If you cannot spare the money today, why do you think you will have it in the future? As discussed earlier, you become a slave to the lender. As Ben Franklin once said: "Consider what you do when you run up a large debt; you give another power over your liberty. It's better to go to bed supper-less that to arise in debt. Much wealth is wasted in the getting. The folly of spending dissipates many a fortune in the making."

The vice of borrowing often leads to the second vice of lying. Lying about why you are unable to pay back the money borrowed on a timely basis. Not only lying to others, but worse, lying to yourself. For he who accepts his own lies, is susceptible to the lies of others. The debtor's world becomes distorted.

Already In Debt: But let's assume you are there - already heavily in debt. Your debt may include school loans, credit card debt, debt from large medical or dental bills, debt to your parents, etc.

Bankruptcy: Some debts are dischargeable in bankruptcy. However, changes to the federal bankruptcy laws have made it more difficult (or sometimes even impossible) to get certain debts discharged, such as college loans, child support, restitution for crimes you committed, and even some credit card debt.

Nevertheless, if the bulk of your debt is from medical bills, a business deal gone badly, or a lawsuit not involving a deliberate tort on your part, the bulk of your debt could be wiped out in bankruptcy. This is a very specialized area and varies somewhat from state to state, so if you think bankruptcy might be a viable option, the best advice is to discuss the matter with a local bankruptcy attorney.

Otherwise: The secret to getting out of debt is to take responsibility for your life, to get control over your spending habits and your debt.

Borrowing Over Time: Most people who are heavily in debt got that way by borrowing more and more over many years. Very often such borrowing is a result of spending more than they make. When their credit card balance is approaching their maximum credit line, they simply apply for a new credit card. All too often such uncontrolled spending is the result of trying to impress other people.

An Example: Dick and Jane have very large credit card debts. Dick and Jane explained how they got there: "Our friends had new cars and we felt we deserved new cars also. Our friends went on expensive trips, and we felt we should do likewise. When Dick bought a new motorcycle, Jane felt she was justified in buying a new refrigerator, even though the old one was working just fine. When Dick bought a larger TV, Jane spent a similar amount on jewelry. We now realize that all these expenditures were unnecessary and merely contributed to our debt.

A major reason why so many young people get heavily in debt is that they want to live the same life style as their parents, without having to put in the years of working and saving for that lifestyle.

The result is massive debt. Dick and Jane have almost $120,000 of debt, including outstanding college loans, car loans, credit card debt, and $20,000 owed to Jane's parents who have bailed them out of financial trouble a couple of times.

Dick and Jane rent an apartment and have little hope of ever buying a house, even though Jane's parents offered to help them with the down payment. They had even applied for a home mortgage and they were told that they would have to pay off $50,000 of their debts before they would qualify.

Because of the high interest rate on most of their debt, they can barely make the minimum payments, much less reduce the principal by any significant amount."

Dick and Jane worry a lot about their financial situation. Unfortunately, worry is like a rocking chair. It gives you something to do, but it won't take you anywhere.

How They Got There: One of the principles of getting out of debt is to first understand how you got there in the first place. If Dick and Jane spent only $10 per day more than they earn, that alone can result in very substantial debt. Just $10 per day, a couple of Starbucks and a bagel, for 365 days, amounts to $3,650 per year. Let's see how such a small amount of over spending can amount to $78,000 of debt after eight years if financed on a credit card charging 24% per year.

In the following chart, the interest is calculated on the sum of the prior year balance and the over-spending for the current year; and the ending balance is the prior year's ending balance, plus the current years over spending, plus the interest:

Year	Begin. Balance	Amount Overspent	Interest @ 24%	Ending Balance
1	0	3,650	438	4,088
2	4,088	3,650	1,419	9,157
3	9,157	3,650	2,636	15,443
4	15,443	3,650	4,144	23,237
5	23,237	3,650	6,015	32,902
6	32,902	3,650	8,334	44,886
7	44,886	3,650	11,211	59,747
8	59,747	3,650	14,777	78,175

And then in year eight, the annual interest on $78,175 at 24% is $18,762 per year - or over $1,500 per month! All from "financing" $10 per day on a credit card!

For most people with large debt, they got there in a manner very similar to the above example. It may not have been Starbucks, and it probably didn't happen in the same amount each year. But as you can see, accumulating debt is like a snowball rolling down a hill – it gets larger and faster the further it travels.

Traditional Debt Management: Many debt counselors will tell you to create a budget, which is merely a listing all of the expenses you expect to incur during the coming months. I think that can be helpful, but many people who create a budget then feel justified in spending the amount they put into the budget whether they really need to spend it or not.

Dick and Jane had tried the traditional budget. Unfortunately they viewed the budget as "permission" to spend that much. For instance, they had budgeted $150 per month for dinners out. So they felt it was okay to go out to restaurants several times early in the month. After all, it was there in their budget. But, of course, they shot right through the $150 by the middle of the month, and when friends called later in the month to go out to dinner, what could they say?

It's helpful to prepare a budget because it should force you to review where you spend your money during the past several months. That used to be an easy task years ago when you could just go to your checkbook and list all the entries. Today you not only have to look at each check, but also each credit card statement. Also, it used to be if you spent money in one place, you knew what it was for.

But today, that $475.86 charge at Sam's Club could be for almost anything, and more than likely was for a number of different categories of items, such as some food, an article or two of clothing, dishwasher soap, dog food, and a couple of DVD's. Few people keep those receipts for long, so for the average person to go back and try to figure out what he spent his money on months ago is almost impossible. So what should you do?

You could at least estimate how much you have spent in each category. One interesting technique that might be helpful is to categorize your items as you check out and pay. For instance, you could put your clothes together, then your groceries. Or put your most expensive items first. That way, when you look at your receipt it will be easier to estimate how much was spent by category.

The Best Method: But the REAL SECRET to getting control of your everyday expenses - the ones that often contribute to that $10 per day of overspending - is to create a log of your expenses. Every night you are required to log in what you spent that day. Every night. Let me repeat, EVERY NIGHT!

Include everything that costs more than a dollar, and regardless of whether you paid cash or charged it. If it was at Walmart, you must account for the total by category, such as food, clothing, household items, etc. Furthermore, knowing that you have to account for the expense often discourages spending the money.

It takes some work at first, but usually by the third week it becomes much easier. It is also helpful to carry a file card with you each day to keep track of cash and other expenses. If you will log in all expenses and account for every dollar you spent in a month, it will most likely become obvious where you need to cut back to save.

An Example: Willard got off to the right start after graduating from college. He was afraid that with his "sudden wealth" (a good job), much of it would slip through his fingers. So he kept track of every dime he spent for two months.

Certain patterns became clear. First, he observed that he was spending far too much on alcoholic beverages, especially in bars. To solve this problem, he did two things. First, before going out he would usually have a beer or two at home. Beer at home cost about 50 cents versus $4.00 at the nightclub. Secondly, he would drink a glass of water or coffee between each beer. Not only did he save money, but he also was in better condition to drive home.

The second thing he noticed which he could control was the amount of money he was spending in restaurants, especially lunch. A group at work usually went out for lunch. Willard decided to just quit the group lunches. He used several excuses, such as being behind in his work, or that he packed his lunch today and don't want it to go stale. By avoiding lunches he was able to not only save considerable money and get more work completed, but he also lost five pounds!

Also The Big Expenditures: So far we have emphasized watching those small expenses. But watch the big ones as well. Willard was quite surprised how much it cost to buy a new car. It wasn't just the $25,000 price tag. What surprised him was the amount of sales tax ($1,500) and the registration fee ($500).

The dealer had assured him that he didn't have to worry about these; they would just add them to his car loan. The dealer made it sound like Willard didn't even have to pay them, but of course not only did Willard have to pay for them, but also with interest! In addition, his automobile insurance premium increased somewhat.

After owning the car for five years, the car loan was paid off. Willard considered buying a new car. But his current car was adequate, it was in good shape, and his annual license fee had dropped down to $100. Also, his car insurance was now less because of the age of my car. The result: Willard kept the car for another six years before buying a new one."

Another Example: Remember Dick and Jane. Dick had recently bought a new car and had large car payments. Why did he buy a new car when he was so heavily in debt?

He stated that he had just paid off his old car, and it looked like it was going to need new brakes and tires, and before he spent all that money, he decided to look at new cars. The salesman told him that with the new models coming out shortly, the dealership was literally giving last year's models away. Dick said it was a deal he just couldn't pass up. So he bought it.

What do you tell someone who gets their financial advice of a car salesman?

Priorities In Debt Reduction: In addition to making a list of all your monthly expenses, also make a list of all your assets (and their values) and all your debts (the outstanding balance and the interest rate). This is important in calculating your net worth as discussed earlier in this book. Reviewing your net worth periodically will help provide the motivation to continue your debt reduction program.

Several important principles are involved in debt reduction. Which debts should you pay off first? First, it's important to make all of your payments on time. That will keep or improve your credit rating and may permit you to later obtain lower interest rate credit cards.

After you have made timely payments for 6 months to a year, consider calling your credit card companies to see if they will reduce your interest rate. Some actually will lower your rate. Which ones will do that? You won't know until you ask!

Next, pay off those debts with the highest interest rates. Consider selling off assets which you don't use or which you can't afford. If you are behind in some of your payments, contact the creditor and explain to them your predicament, and try to work out a payment plan to get back on schedule and to at least stop all those late charges.

But Don't Do This: Some people, when determined to get out of debt, cut up all their credit cards, and, although there is something to be said for that approach, it doesn't, of course, cancel the debt. Moreover, a credit card is nice to have for convenience as well as for an emergency. It's almost impossible to rent a car without a credit card. It's inconvenient to buy gasoline without a credit card.

So, cut up most of your credit cards, but keep one or two for convenience and emergencies, just don't use them every day. Many people find that when the pay cash, they are more careful about what they buy. And if they don't have the cash, they don't buy it.

Mental Preparation: Be content with what you have. The entire media industry is designed to make you dissatisfied with what you have so you will buy something else. The average American watches television over 30 hours per week. There are 25 commercials in the average hour of watching. That's 750 commercials per week! Newspapers are typically over 50% ads; news magazine, 50% ads, magazines like People or Cosmopolitan, close to 70% ads.

Most web sites you visit also bombard you with ads.

Combine those ads with radio on the way to work, billboards, and the like, and you are probably exposed to over 1,500 ads per week.

One way to help you get out of debt is to simply reduce your exposure to such ads.

Also avoid the shopping malls Avoid shopping online. If you need something, go to a store or a website that sells only that item; don't go to the mall where you will be exposed to more ads, to more temptation. Studies have shown that the more time people spend shopping, the more they buy.

Most importantly, don't even go shopping unless there is something you absolutely need. A new dress would not fall into the category of something you absolutely need. What would qualify? Food, toilet paper, and the like. Get the picture!

Convenience Not The Only Factor: Willard (Mr. Frugal discussed earlier!) doesn't mind paying 10% to 20% more at Walgreens than he would pay for the same item at Walmart. Willard can go into Walgreens, find his $5.00 item, and leave - all within ten minutes. If he goes into Walmart, not only does it take a lot longer to get in and out, but he always seems to buy another $20.00 worth of stuff he does not really need.

Avoid Borrowing: Consider borrowing for only two items: education and a home. Yes, there are circumstances under which borrowing for a car might make sense. But if you are in debt, and must borrow to buy a car, consider buying, for example, a three year old car with a three year loan, rather than a new car with a seven year loan. Once the car is paid off, don't buy another one until you absolutely have to.

Other than the items mentioned above, don't borrow to buy anything. I asked Jane if she would borrow money to buy a dress, and she said, "Of course not." But isn't that what she is doing when she buys a dress with a credit card when she knows it is unlikely that she will be able to pay off the entire credit card balance at the end of the month?

The credit card companies make it very easy for you to borrow money at high interest rates to buy things you don't really need. Even if the interest rate doesn't seem high at first, ("0% interest for six months!"), after the introductory period, or if you are late making a payment or two, the interest rate could exceed 20%!

The credit industry is fueled to a large extent by our ignorance of our spending habits and the true cost of borrowing. If we really knew how much we were paying on our debt, we would be less inclined to incur it.

Pay Off Debt First: Dick wondered if he should continue making contributions to his 401(k) plan at work. Dick's 401(k) is earning 6%. Why should he invest at 6% when he is paying 24% on his credit cards?

For every $1,000 of credit card debt he is paying $240 in interest each year while earning only $60 on the $1,000 in his 401(k). That doesn't make any sense at all. Whatever is being deducted from his payroll for his 401(k) contribution should be immediately diverted to paying off his credit cards.

There Is One Exception: If Dick's employer matches his contribution, say up to 3% of his salary, he should contribute that 3% because the employer matching contribution is like an instant 100% return on his investment. That contribution makes sense even if he is heavily in debt.

If Dick is allowed to borrow from his 401(k) plan, he should consider doing so to pay off his expensive credit cards. Dick needs to be careful that he doesn't spend the borrowed money or run up his credit card balance again.

A Word Of Caution: Beware of debt counselors and "consolidators". Most of these folks seem sympathetic, then scare you, then offer an easy solution for a fee. Once you have paid an upfront fee, they have little motivation to help you and you are back trying to help yourself with fewer resources than you had before. Am I suggesting that most of these offers are scams? Yes, and they prey on people in debt looking for an easy way out.

You can figure these things for yourself without paying someone who makes it sound easy with their system. With careful monitoring of your debts and spending habits, you can get out of debt. But don't stop there. Continue on that same course to build your wealth.

In this chapter we helped you get out of debt, or at least scared you enough to avoid ever getting heavily into debt. The next chapter will discuss the second important element to wealth accumulation, and that is maximizing income.

***

Maximizing Your Income

"The key to maximizing your earnings is to develop highly marketable skills. Rather than being a 'Jack of All Trades,' be a master of one."

Definition Of Income: By income, we mean the payment you receive for work performed. This could be your salary, your commissions, or the profits from your own business. It is important to realize that all a person possesses to generate income is his or her talent, education, time, and labor.

Lost Income: If you waste a day at the shopping center when you could be working, not only are you likely to waste money buying things you don't really need, but you have foregone the opportunity to earn more money as well. But is there no time for leisure?

Leisure: I do not mean to down play the importance of leisure time. The diligent man makes his life better by how he uses his leisure time. Laziness and idleness are the opposite of leisure. Don't confuse the two. Leisure is time for fixing up your house, exercising your mind or your body, reading a good book (this one??).

Leisure is time for planning your future; leisure is time for revitalizing yourself and your family. Time is not to be wasted. Time lost is never found.

The efficient person plans his leisure carefully; makes the most of it, and then has something to show for it. The idle person lets time pass without a benefit. As time is what life is made of, wasting time is nothing more than partial suicide.

Too many people die at an old age, having lived but half a life. Time is a form of wealth that, regardless of how it is invested, you have less remaining at the end of each day. Make the most of your life.

Stayed Employed: Losing your job because of a poor attitude or a dishonest act is like killing a racehorse. Not only do you lose its future winnings, but you also lose its stud fees in retirement and the many generations of winners the racehorse is likely to produce. It's like killing the proverbial goose that laid the golden egg. He who murders a dollar also murders all that it might have grown to.

Developing highly marketable skills can be accomplished through formal education, specific technical training, or on-the- job training. More often than not, it is a combination of these methods.

The key is to offer your employer or your customer a product or service which no one else can offer, or at least one which is superior to other such products or services on the market.

If you are an employee, perform your job in such a manner that your employer feels that you are helping the company maximize its profit. That means going out of your way to do the best job you can. If you are in a service or sales business, that means making sure the customer is satisfied. If you work for a large organization, that means making your boss look good.

Avoid A Lay-Off: John, a middle manager for a large telecom-munications company, reported: "I had survived the first two lay-offs (reduction in workforce) at our company. It seemed funny that the company was doing well, but still had periodic lay-offs. I asked my boss about this and he explained that he was pretty sure that periodic lay-off was the company's way of getting rid of less productive employees without firing them.

Being laid off is less offensive to the employee than being fired. Laid-off employees are less likely to sue the company."

Education: Formal education is often the key to getting out of poverty. Immigrants usually understand this more than the equally poor who have lived in this country for many years and have adopted a victim mentality. That's why the children of Asian immigrants often become very successful professionals, whereas those raised here in poverty seem to make little effort to help themselves; education to them means learning how to apply for government welfare programs.

Finishing high school and graduating from college usually requires sacrifices. Not just the time sacrifices of going to class, studying hard, and often learning about things you might never use, but also the financial sacrifices of delaying entering the job market, living somewhat frugally as a student, and perhaps taking out student loans which must be repaid.

An employer once told me that he preferred to hire college graduates simply because there was concrete evidence that they would finish something they started, that they did things they didn't necessarily want to do. One of the most valuable lessons of college is that the person develops the ability to make himself do a thing which he has to do, when it ought to be done, and regardless of whether or not he wants to do it.

Examples: Sam was raised in New England. He majored in accounting, and hated history, but did find the story of the Alamo and Texas independence of particular interest. One of his first job interviews upon graduating was in New York City with a gentleman who mentioned that he was originally from San Antonio (home of the Alamo). Sam and the interviewer discussed the Alamo and Texas in general for over twenty minutes.

Sam did receive a job offer from the company, and although he did not accept it, Sam suspected that his interest in the Alamo may have been part of the reason for the job offer.

Ivan majored in biology in college in the early 1970's, and planned to go into teaching. A friend suggested that he might enjoy taking a course in computer programming. Ivan really had no interest in computers at the time, but he took the course anyway, and learned the rudiments of programming in simple BASIC language.

Several years later while teaching he wrote a program in BASIC that would run on a personal computer and would help him administer and grade multiple-choice tests. It became a popular program at his school and several teachers starting using it.

A few years later Ivan was recruited by a computer software company to be in charge of developing software for the educational market. Interestingly, although he was in charge of product design, he never was involved with programming again. The company was very successful, and having joined the company early in its startup phase, his stock options and the like allowed Ivan to retire fairly wealthy at 55 years of age.

Maria's father was always a stickler for grammar. He was from Spain and Maria was raised in a bilingual family. In college she majored in Spanish, and soon after graduating she sent her resume to a company looking for a bilingual (Spanish) administrative assistant. A representative of the company called her in for an interview, which subsequently led to an offer that Maria accepted.

Several years later her boss confided in Maria the reason why the offer was made to her rather that several other equally qualified candidates:

"When I first called you and said, 'I would like to speak with Maria', you said, 'This is she.' The three other candidates replied, 'This is her.' Your grammatically-correct 'this is she' resulted in my viewing you initially more favorably."

The company was Microsoft, and even as a lower managerial employee, Maria received stock options and participated in other company plans, and now has over $2 million of company stock. Her father is deceased now, and Maria's only regret is that she never thanked him for being a grammar freak!

Of course, education can be achieved in many ways, not just through college. Trade schools and on-the-job training (or should I say on the job learning!) are often just as effective. Fortune favors the prepared mind.

James: "As a teenager I worked for Mr. Ortega in his lawn mowing business. Mr. Ortega not only taught me how to mow a yard efficiently, but also how to set, clean, and maintain my mower. Although he employed several of us, each of us was assigned a specific mower for which we were responsible.

He also taught me what it took to keep customers pleased. One customer, Mrs. Jones, in particular, spoke very highly of Mr. Ortega. I asked Mr. Ortega why she seemed so pleased with his yard service, and he explained how he first obtained her as a customer:

'She was having a party Saturday night and called me Saturday morning, explaining that she needed to have her yard mowed that afternoon. I had never met her before, but had mowed a neighbor's yard. It had rained for several days before and the grass was somewhat overgrown and still wet.

I went to her house and explained to her the difficulty of mowing her yard, the need to frequently clean the mower and the extra time required. I told her that I would be glad to work on her yard, but because of the condition and wetness, I would have to cut it high (meaning it would probably need to be cut again in less than a week), I would need to clean the wet grass out of the mower every few minutes.

I apologized for the charge, but because of the extra time it would take, I would need to charge her about three times what it would normally cost. She told to me that her existing service company didn't want to do it, but reluctantly quoted her about the same price, but didn't explain why. She thought they were price gouging her because she was desperate to have her yard mowed for her party. She was clearly irritated by them.

My explanation made sense to her and she agreed to have me mow her yard. Not only did I mow her yard, but I also edged a section of the sidewalk that looked uneven. It only took me a few minutes, but she noticed that I was doing it, and actually gave me a tip in addition to my large charge for mowing the yard. She was very pleased with how her yard looked for her party.

Mr. Ortega was a great teacher. He taught me that people aren't just paying to have the top inch of grass cut. They were paying for the appearance of their yard. If weeds appear, we would spot spray that area. If a brown area appeared, we would fertilize and suggest extra watering. We kept the customers advised about all we were doing to care for their yards.

I learned from Mr. Ortega that the best formula for success is to under promise and over deliver.

I worked for Mr. Ortega for over two years before our family moved to a neighboring town. I decided that I would start my own lawn care business. I purchased a used mower at a garage sale and was soon in business.

I called Mr. Ortega to let him know what I was doing and to thank him for teaching me so much about the business. He offered to lend me some money to buy another mower, and edger, and additional equipment. He even went to Home Depot with me to select the equipment.

Soon I had several employees and had repaid Mr. Ortega. The following winter I expanded into snow removal and ground level tree and shrub trimming. While friends were watching TV in the evenings and on weekends, I was expanding my business.

I remember going up to one house to ask the owner if he could use my services. I had remembered from Mr. Ortega that it is best to approach new customers when their grass needed mowing. The owner went into a tirade about how he had no interest in a service contract, and that he usually enjoyed mowing his own lawn and didn't need me.

Although I usually operate on service contracts, even if informal, I offered to mow his yard only upon his request and without any contract. I pointed out to him that his yard was in need of mowing and that apparently, even though he enjoyed mowing his yard, he obviously had not found time to do it over the weekend. I offered to mow it the next day at a fair price, and told him he had no obligation to ever use my services ever again. He agreed.

Apparently he didn't enjoy mowing his yard that much, as my company has mowed his yard every other week for the past three years!

I now have ten employees and take care of over 200 personal residences and business properties. Last year I made over $100,000 from my business."

For James, on the job training with a mentor, someone who would go out of his way to help him, proved invaluable. James never went to college, but by 30 years of age, was making more than most college graduates his age, and, perhaps, even more than his old boss, Mr. Ortega.

In the next chapter we will explore the importance of college, the importance of your major field of study, the cost of that education, and the impact of student loans.

***

Education as an Investment

"To get a good-paying job, get a good education."
– Sign in a Boston Subway Station

Education, be it learning from experiences or learning from a formal curriculum, begins at birth and generally continues until death. We learn not to put our fingers on a hot range either from others or from personal experience. Life is a continual learning process, but it is our exposure to formal education early in life that often determines our financial future.

On Average: It's no secret that the average college graduate today can expect to earn over one million dollars more than the average high school graduate. But does that mean that all college graduates will earn more than all high school graduates? Of course not, as many factors go into determining what your earnings will be over the next five, ten, and even twenty years.

Attending college was very frustrating for George. He told his father that he felt that he would never need or use 90% of what he was learning. Much to his surprise, his father agreed with him, but his father pointed out that although that is true, you never know in advance which 10% will be helpful in life, and the larger the body of knowledge you acquire, the larger that 10%.

We never know in advance what might be most important. For many, a college education is actually cheap. It's the lack of a college education that can be expensive.

Follow Your Dreams: What are you interested in? What particular aptitudes do you have? Often, those may determine your career. But such aptitudes still need to be refined. The person who likes to build things has many career options. He may end up being a construction worker, a construction engineer, or an architect. Each occupation has its own educational and physical requirements and its own rewards.

When Johnny was six years old, his parents took him to see the Harlem Globetrotters play basketball. Johnny told his parents that he really wanted to play basketball when he grew up. He played every chance he had at his local Y.M.C.A. and at school. Johnny played on his school team in middle school.

But as other boys grew taller, Johnny at five foot four inches found that his physical limitations limited his competitive abilities. But he never gave up totally on his love of the sport. He took aptitude tests while in school and eventually went into sports management. So follow your dreams, but be practical also.

Factors: What are some of the factors that will affect your earnings ten years out of school? The school you attend, its reputation for your field of study, your major, your grade point average, and where you choose to live.

Selecting A College: One strategy for career development is to consider the school's reputation. The better the school, the more income you are likely to earn over the next decade or two.

Obtaining an M.B.A. degree from the Harvard Business School will likely open more doors and with a larger salary than the same degree from Arizona State University.

No one school is outstanding in every field. For instance, Cornell University is widely recognized to have an outstanding degree program in hotel management. But its program in marine biology is inferior to a similar program offered at the University of Hawaii. Determine what you want to major in, and then go to the best school for that major that you can afford.

Selecting A Major: So does that mean that you have to decide on a major your first year? No, but by the beginning of your second year, you should have a pretty good idea of the course of study you wish to pursue. At many schools, the first year will cover many of the basic requirements for any degree program.

So, regardless of what major you end up pursuing, and even if you transfer to another college, those first year courses will count toward your degree, and may well help prepare you for your advanced courses.

For instance, being able to communicate clearly in writing may be important to almost any major. Other courses, such as college algebra, may lay the foundation for many majors where math is important. Just make sure that those first year courses will be credited toward most degrees and are likely to transfer if you change schools.

A specialized study does not mean that you cannot take other courses that are of interest to you. A broad education expands your employment opportunities, regardless of your major. Twenty years after graduating, at least one-third of such graduates are employed in a field other than their major. For example, one of the governors of Colorado (John Hickenlooper) is a former geologist. One never knows where life will take them. Luck favors the prepared mind.

Where will the best job opportunities be in the future? As the country ages, those specializing in health care will be in high demand, whether nurse, doctor, or lab technician. Government employment, which was often shunned because of low salaries by the older generation, may be another area to consider, given the better pay, the job security, and the employee benefits.

Geographic Location: If you plan to stay in your area of the country, that may limit, or at least help refine, your target occupation. If this is your goal, visit local employers to determine the best school to attend and the best courses to take. Valuable information can be obtained by talking to local employers even during your first year of college! Your initial information seeking interviews may open the door for a real job interview several years later. Such networking should be developed long before it is needed.

For example, if you hope to never leave Vermont, then petroleum engineering can probably be eliminated from your list. Similarly, resort management could be placed near the top of your list of possibilities. One Vermont student had discussions with several local resort human resources managers who told him that too many graduates lacked knowledge of both financial accounting and United States history. Given that student's career plans in resort management, do you think such information could be helpful to him in planning his college curriculum?

Unemployment Rates: One might think that the unemployment rate would be greater among higher paid professions, but just the opposite is true. Those in higher earning professions earn more simply because there is more demand than supply. Using Google you can get some ideas on first year earnings identified by major as well as employment opportunities in your own geo-politic area of the country.

Beware Of Averages: In some professions the earnings are pretty much level for all persons with similar education and years on the job. While school teachers in New York City earn considerably more than those in Lincoln, Nebraska, the difference is not that significant when adjusted for the cost of living and additional taxes.

Moreover, ten years out of school, 90% of the school teachers probably earn within 10% of the average earnings for all teachers who are ten years out of school, after adjustments for location and the like. On the other hand, 90% of the acting majors earn far less than the average for such majors, simply because a very few earn millions more than the average, thus distorting the average toward the high side.

Similarly, the average income for those graduating with an (Masters in Business Administration) needs to be further refined when comparing the Harvard M.B.A. program with a similar program at South Dakota State University. So be somewhat skeptical of, but don't ignore, the "averages".

Starting Salaries: Before making a decision about your major while in college, consider the likely earnings as well as your interest in the work required to obtain that degree. Certain majors may require more work than others, but you may find the extra work at nineteen years of age results in twice the salary at 25 years of age. Treat college as an investment.

All too often students select majors based upon how "easy" the major is - how likely they are to stay in school and not flunk out. It's no secret that many students attending college will never complete a degree program, and such students are likely to earn only slightly more than the average worker at McDonald's. Ironically, education is the one thing that many people pay big bucks for, and then try to get as little for their investment as possible!

Although colleges tend to downplay the financial success of graduates in their various fields of study, you shouldn't. At many schools, whether you major in electrical engineering or in sociology, the tuition is the same. But the starting salaries for graduates in each course of study are vastly different.

The average starting salary for an electrical engineering graduate is over $80,000; for a sociology graduate, under $40,000. Moreover, unemployment among social science workers is far greater than electrical engineers. But even the sociology graduate will earn more than the college dropout working at Walmart. For someone working full time (2,000 hours per year) at a minimum wage job paying $10 per hour, his annual earnings would be only $20,000.

Business administration majors come in somewhere in between at about $50,000. Even within business administration, accounting majors tend to earn far more that those who major in marketing.

A student majoring in photography is likely to earn less than half of what a nurse makes the first year after graduation, as well as ten years later, with unemployment higher in photography than nursing.

At many schools, both the nursing major and the engineering major can take one course in photography that will count toward their degree. So you can take a course or two about which you are passionate, while still majoring in a higher paying course of study.

College Is Not For Everyone: Perhaps by now you were anticipating that this chapter would lecture about the advantages of college, and urge everyone to attend and select a well-paying major. To the contrary, far more people are attending college today than probably should be.

College is an investment of time, money, and delayed earnings. For many that investment makes sense. For instance, you cannot become an attorney, a doctor, or even a school teacher without a college degree.

The post-high school educational system has experienced "Grade Inflation" over the past several decades. It used to be that "C" was average. Just as many students would receive a "B" (above average) as received a "D" (below average). It was referred to as a bell curve.

More recently, as survey of schools found that 80% of the grades were either "A" or "B". Accordingly, you could be a below average student and still have a "B" average – or 3.0 grade point.

Gresham's law was originally applied to money stating that the bad drives out the good. For example, the government stopped issuing quarters made of silver in 1964. All coins after that year were copper clad with far less metallic value. Soon thereafter almost all the silver coins disappeared from circulation.

Similarly, grade inflation has reduced the value of what used to be an above-average grade point, and has caused many employers to put less emphasis on the student's grade point average, and even less emphasis on the college degree.

It's sad to say, but many college students have, in effect, been misled. College is not for everyone, and given that rapid rise in tuition and other costs over the past two decades, college is not a good investment for a fairly large percentage of the students now attending college.

So, if you are considering college, or perhaps an advanced degree, weigh the cost/benefits carefully. Treat education as an investment from which you expect an above average return.

Loans: Student loans are another factor to consider. Many students go to school and take out large student loans to cover their living costs, such as an off-campus apartment, car, and other luxuries for a college student. Consider how many years it will take for you to pay off those loans at the salary you expect to earn. If you must borrow, borrow only for necessities.

For the average sociology graduate, the meager starting salary will leave very little after loan repayments for basic living expenses. The engineering student, on the other hand, may be able to pay back similar loans in just a few years.

For some students, college is a way to borrow money to live on while they are unemployed. It is a temporary "easy way out" for those who are less motivated about their studies, but are reluctant to enter the job market. Those students are unlikely to get decent jobs upon graduating (if they ever do), and will be saddled with large student loans that will haunt them most of their adult life.

The "easy way out" often proves very difficult to live with later on. Defaulting on student loans can result in your wages being garnished or in your being turned down for a home loan.

Student loans are non-dischargeable in bankruptcy, so they will continue to haunt you for the rest of your life. There are many retired persons today who are having a portion of their social security check withheld to repay such loans taken out decades ago.

Think twice about taking out such loans. Use them only for necessities of obtaining that degree. Don't hock your future for a life of luxury as a student, especially if your major will likely lead to lower-paying employment. Borrow only for essentials!

Technical Training: Consider vocational or technical training as well. Plumbers, electricians, carpenters, and welders usually earn above average incomes. Training, combined with an apprenticeship, may well offer you greater financial rewards than a college degree in a low-paying major, especially if you have the aptitude for working with your hands.

You can start earning money sooner, and many such jobs cannot be "exported" overseas and thus offer greater job security than certain other occupations.

Schools are recognizing this and are beginning to offer courses in the trades again. John attended a local community college to learn welding. He reported, "Welders earn good money. After several years of working as a welder, I was promoted to maintenance supervisor. I suspect I am earning far more than my average classmate who completed community college with a traditional education."

Technical training for many persons is a viable alternative to traditional college. Talking with local employers can often give you a better idea of the technical training that will offer you the best job opportunities for the time and monetary investment involved. This is a great option for those with the aptitude for such employment.

The Military: Another alternative to college is joining the military. Not only does the military train one to be disciplined and organized, but many skills learned in the service are transferable to similar jobs in civilian life.

Susan, who was trained as a sonar operator on a naval destroyer, later landed a job as a flight controller. Much of her training in sonar operations was equally applicable to radar operations. The recommendation from her commanding officer was also quite helpful to her in securing civilian employment.

Moreover, the military offers transition programs as well as tuition assistance in pursuing formal education. So joining the military does not rule out college, but, often, merely postpones college until you can better afford it and, perhaps, your career goals are more firmly established.

Continuing Education: Many graduates, from either high school or college, are able to improve their earning abilities by attending continuing education programs during the evenings or over weekends. If you work in accounting, work toward an accounting degree if you don't already have one. If you are in sales, take a "Dale Carnegie" course or a similar program to enhance your selling skills. If you are a teacher, obtaining a master's degree may qualify you for a promotion, or at least higher pay.

Self Help: Lastly, a person can become a reasonably educated person on his or her own. Check out textbooks at your local library. Read extensively. On your own you can learn a considerable amount about almost any subject. There are even free (or very low cost) internet programs that can help virtually anyone become an educated person. If the average person would spend just 50% of the time he or she spends watching television watching educational programs (instead of football, soap operas, movies, and the like), that person could become just as educated as most college graduates. Once you are in your last year of college, you will be looking for your first well-paying job, and the next chapter attempts to help you get – and keep – that job.

***

Getting – And Keeping – That First Real Job

"I am a great believer in luck. I find that the harder I work, the luckier I get. Success usually comes to those who are too busy to be looking for it." - Thomas Jefferson

Once you are nearing the completion of your formal education, be it high school or college, you will be seeking your first fulltime, well-paying job. You will be completing job applications, sending out resumes, and networking with friends and family to locate that ideal job.

Anyone searching for a job would benefit from reading the Bible on this topic, <u>What Color is your Parachute?</u> By Richard N. Bolles. This book has been rewritten and updated many times since it was first published in 1970, and the more recent editions include extensive advice on using social media when searching for employment. It would be very difficult to add much to that very thorough treatise on the topic of the job search. So we will cover just a few of the basics here.

Job Applications: You will undoubtedly complete many job applications while seeking employment. Get used to it, but don't get sloppy. Many employers like to see an applicant's handwritten application. Is it written clearly? A sloppy writer often does sloppy work, if for no other reason than he can't read his own notes. Write as clearly as you can, even though it may take a little longer.

Your application will be your first (and possibly your last) chance to make a favorable impression on your prospective employer.

Does the applicant use proper punctuation, sentence structure, and the like? Can the applicant read and answer questions appropriately? Are you accurate? An employer must wonder about the applicant who indicates he graduated from high school in 2007, but started college in 2005. If you actually took college courses in high school, then a further explanation would be appropriate on the application, or else the interviewer may view you as either inaccurate or misleading.

Read the application carefully as you complete it. If it asks for your educational achievements in chronological order, don't list your college work before your high school. Employers often use applications to filter out those who don't know how to follow instructions.

When finished, reread your application (and resume) from this employer's viewpoint. If you were the employer, would you even ask this person in for an interview? Hint: If possible, make copies of the application before completing it so that if you do make an error, or decide to reword something, you will have a clean application with which to work.

Also make copies of whatever you submit to a prospective employer. If you are called in for an interview, you can review in advance what your interviewer is looking at during the interview and perhaps anticipate what questions he or she may have.

Resumes: Job seekers often think of resumes as door openers. They think it offers a chance to present all their qualities, and on paper where they can't be, at least initially, questioned. But employers often think of resumes as disqualifiers.

If an employer has one hundred resumes for one job, what is the first thing the employer does? The employer skims them looking not for the most qualified applicant, but initially with the goal of discarding all but a select few. Will yours be one of the few that are selected for further review?

So how can your resume survive this initial screening process? There are a number of factors that can result in immediate rejection. A picture of yourself is usually inappropriate, unless you are applying for a modeling job. Don't be too sloppy or use a poor or unusual format. Misspelled words, bad grammar, and poorly aligned indentations tell the reviewer that you are a sloppy person. This is what your work will be like.

Don't Be Misleading: More and more employers are checking not only references, but also verifying your actual graduation. So don't be misleading. Also, state accurately both the month and year of your prior employment. Most employers view gaps in employment far less negatively than attempts to be deceptive. The person who only indicates the year(s) of prior employment appears like he is trying to hide periods of unemployment.

Don't be too general in your wording. "I am looking for a job that will allow me to use my skills and offer me a chance for advancement." Not only is that a "me" oriented statement, but it is trite. It certainly does not tell the employer why you might be good for the job.

On the other hand, don't be too creative. Hard to read fonts, such as italics, multiple fonts (use no more than two), graphics, pictures of your pet, may make your resume stand out, but in a negative way.

Use A Resume That Addresses The Job: So how can you be creative, not trite, but not too creative? Think about the job and what the employer might be looking for an employee and what their concerns might be. Research the industry, the company, and the job.

Poor Julie. She was approaching graduation from college and knew she had to start applying for employment. She had majored in physical education; her grade point was mediocre; her only work experience had been working at McDonald's. In her spare time she played computer games. She wasn't even sure what kind of work she might enjoy.

Julie loved to travel and thought it would be great to work for an airline. She saw an employment ad for "an airline customer service representative." Julie spent a couple of days researching the job and the company. She even went to at the local airport to discuss what a "customer service representative does with several airline employees. "That's ticker counter work – that's what I do!" one employee said.

"What are some of the things a ticket counter person does?" Julie asked. Briefly, the employee responded, "We deal with passengers; we issue tickets; we use our computers to check people in; we check in their bags. We work different times of the day and being on time is very important."

Julie's Resume: Julie modified her resume somewhat based upon this new information, but it was her opening statement that got her the job interview: "My goal is to work for an airline, and customer service would be a great place to start. My experience in shift work at the counter at McDonald's for two years during college has trained me to be both fast and courteous, deal with irate customers, and handle money transactions accurately."

"I learn new computers systems easily, and my weight lifting in college has taught me how to lift without injuring myself. My participation in sports at school has taught me the importance of teamwork."

After reading that opening statement on her resume, do you think the employer even cares much about her education, other work experience, her grade point, and the like? If the remainder of the resume looks even average, this applicant goes to the top of the list. This resume is not about "me" - the employee - but about the employer and the job. Research the company, the industry, and the specific job requirements.

Julie has memorized most of the cities that this airline served and from which major airports. From her conversations with airline employees at the airport, she knew the problems the airlines had during bad weather. She even watched the original "Airport" movie before her interview.

During the interview she even commented that her Suburu had four-wheel drive and could get her to the airport even in a blizzard. Her resume got her the interview, but her burning desire for the job – including her enthusiasm and advanced preparation – got her the job offer!

What are some of the other traits that employers are looking for? A few might be loyalty, honesty, work ethic, commitment, fitting in. Most employers would rather hire someone who is "average" who will stay with the company for five years than a "star" who will leave in five months. They would rather hire the "average" applicant who will work well with the other employees, than a "star" who is difficult to work with.

If you are applying at a local company, emphasize that you grew up in the area, family here, and are not interested in being relocated. If you have only had one job for several years, emphasize your loyalty to your past employer.

Multiple Resumes: There is nothing wrong with having several different resumes; in fact, it would usually be advisable. Isn't it worth a few extra minutes if it helps you get the job you want? Or need! The resume that addresses the particular job, industry, or location will get more attention than those that don't.

In fact, if you don't customize your resume, the resume says (between the lines) "I don't understand what this job entails, I am not sure how my experience and education are relevant, and I don't care what this employer is looking for. I just hope there will be a job there somewhere that I am qualified for." You are asking the employer, who has one hundred resumes to sort through for perhaps one or two jobs, to do your work for you.

To some extent, you can use a cover letter to address such specifics, but if you do, make sure your cover letter is consistent with your resume. Keep your resume and your cover letters in electronic form where they can be easily customized for a specific position or emailed as needed.

One Last Review: So you have just customized your resume and are ready to mail/email it to the employer. Stop. Do one last review. Read the job announcement again. Think about the job, the industry, the company, and the location. Do a little research on the internet. The more you know about the company and the job, the better you can tailor your resume.

Now forget about yourself and pretend you are the employer (perhaps the person who will be your immediate supervisor) reviewing your resume and one hundred other resumes. What can you do to make your resume stand out positively from the rest? Did you relate your experience and education to the job? Did you consider other factors that may be attractive to your prospective employer (boss?) Ask yourself, why would I want to hire this person?

Google your name and see what a prospective employer might see. Better that nothing comes up than your drinking pictures on Facebook. Is there someone with an identical name but a negative background that appears on the first few screens? There is no harm in adding at the end of your resume: "Please note that if you Google my name, the Jane Smith who was arrested in Teaneck, New Jersey, is not me!"

The Employer Calls You: Call yourself from another phone. Listen to your message. Is that what you want a prospective employer to hear? "Out drinking! Leave a message!" will do more harm than a poor resume. Your message should state your name and state that your will return the call promptly. Cutesy messages, loud music, poor grammar, and background noise can all be a turn-off to the prospective employer.

Even if your message is professional sounding, can it be improved? Rerecord the message until it is perfect. If an employer calls, listen to the messages left on your phone. Just returning a call without listening to the message shows poor manners and will likely result in your application being rejected.

The Elevator Speech: Picture this scenario: You just dropped off your resume at a company, and as you are leaving, in the elevator is the director of human resources. He starts a conversation and then says, "Really, which job are you applying for?"

You have only 30 seconds as you travel between the tenth and first floor. What do you say? Develop a 30 second "elevator" speech that summarizes your job search objectives and your qualifications. Practice and refine that speech until it flows naturally.

Attend employment fairs to get ideas on how to better present yourself, even though there may be no employers/jobs there that are of interest to you. Dress appropriately. Ask for comments regarding your resume and your presentation. Practice your elevator speech. Talk to as many people as you can, ask questions, but more importantly, listen, listen, listen.

The New Hire: So now you have been hired and are starting your first "real job." A major factor in your success will be determined by your first few weeks and months at work. So what words of wisdom can be given the new employee to help him or her succeed with a new organization? Because employers and jobs vary so much, it is difficult to offer specific advice. However, here are a few generic pearls of wisdom offered by others:

The First Thirty Days: The first thirty days on the job are the most important. It is during that time that your coworkers develop their initial - and often lasting - impression of you. If you appear to be lazy or incompetent, you will spend the next five years trying to overcome that initial impression. On the other hand, if you initially appear bright, on the ball, industrious, that reputation can carry you through the next five years and even during periods when you are perhaps not so industrious.

Ten Minutes: The ten most important minutes of the day are the five minutes before you are supposed to start work and the five minutes after quitting time. Why do I say that?

Well, the person who is at his job five minutes before starting time and still there five minutes after quitting time is viewed as an ambitious, hard worker by all. But the person who comes in five minutes late and leaves five minutes early is viewed as lazy and less productive.

Expectations: In your first "real job", learn what your boss expects of you. What are the do's and don't do's? How will you be evaluated six months from now? Ask your boss, "If I am doing a good job, what will you be saying to me six months from now? I assume that if I am not doing a good job, I won't even be here six months from now, but what would poor performance look like and how can I avoid it?"

Coworkers: To build a strong career, you will need the recognition and respect of others in your company. Get to know your coworkers. Privately, on a file card or electronic media, make notes about their name, where they are from, their families, and what you discussed with them.

The next time you are scheduled to meet or have lunch with a coworker refer back to your notes. "Did your wife recover from her operation? Are Johnny's grades improving?" such comments show that you are concerned about them, that you listened, and what they said – even about their family – was important. Learn not only from your coworkers and your boss, but also from others who might be good mentors. The more you understand "who does what" in your company, the more effective you will be as an employee and the better chance for advancement.

The Customer: Sam Walton (founder of Walmart): "There is only one boss in this company and that is the customer. He can fire everybody from the chairman on down, simply by deciding to spend his money elsewhere. Anyone who thinks customers are not important should try doing without them for ninety days."

Suggestions: Pay attention to how your coworkers do things. Suggesting ideas on how to improve the way things are done should be handled carefully. Watch how others handle this delicate opportunity. All too often an employee may feel like the suggestion box is fed directly into the paper shredder, but don't give up and don't be offended when your suggestion is ignored. Sometimes a suggestion won't be acted upon for several months.

Don't develop a bad attitude because no one is paying attention to you or your suggestions, and don't be discouraged when your idea is adopted by someone (your boss?) else who gets credit for it. Such things happen, but eventually your efforts will be recognized.

Appearances: In the business world appearance all too often is more important than the quality of your work. Combine both quality work and the appearance of being a go-getter, and you are on your way to your first big promotion. Dress for the position you want, not the position you have.

When you arrive at your job in the morning, let the first thing you say brighten everybody's day. Answer the telephone with enthusiasm and energy in your voice and with a smile upon your face. Some people will even go so far as to put a mirror and a sign saying "Smile before you answer that phone!" in front of their telephone.

Stop what you are doing and look up when anyone approaches your desk. Stand when greeting a person who enters your office or work area. Don't get caught glancing at your watch when you're talking to someone. It's rude and they will be offended. Never admit at work that you are tired, angry, or bored.

Your Boss: The fastest way to get a promotion is to make your boss look good, even if he (or she – they come in both flavors) is an idiot.

Not only will your boss be impressed, but so will other managers. They will think, "Gee, if he can make that jerk look good, he can make me look great!" Thus other people in the company will want you to work for them.

Learn The Trade: Do it right the first time. It takes less time to do a thing right than it does to explain why you did it wrong. Don't waste time learning the "tricks of the trade"; instead, learn the trade. Find something that's important to your company and learn to do it better than anyone else. One key to improving your earning power is to learn to do just a few things very, very, very well. Daily performance is what is most important. You cannot build a reputation on what you are going to do.

Attendance: 80% of success is just showing up. A recent survey showed that over 50% of the employees who were "laid off" or fired were let go because of poor job attendance. Bad habits are developed early in life. The student who skips school is also more likely to skip work.

The discharged employee always has a good sounding reason why he or she were late or absent. "I (or my spouse or child) was sick" or "my car wouldn't start" are two of the most common excuses. But sooner or later, the boss realizes that the company cannot depend on this employee to be at work when needed.

Ironically, many employees who are let go aren't told why. It's easier for the company or department to have a 10% reduction in force to get rid of the deadwood. That way the employer doesn't have to argue about why you were late or other reasons as to why you were "let go".

Volunteering: Volunteer often. Sometimes the jobs no one wants conceal the biggest opportunities. When there is a piano to be moved, don't reach for the stool.

Criticizing: Praise in public; criticize in private, but never criticize the person who signs your paycheck. If you are unhappy with your job, resign; but don't quit your job until you have another job lined up.

Salaries: Don't discuss salaries. If your best friend finds out what you make, one of two things are likely to happen. If you earn less than your friend, your friend will think less of you. If you earn more than your friend, your friend will think you are overpaid, and hope you fail.

As sad as this may sound, it is simply a fact of human nature. Similarly, never discuss money with people who have much less or much more than you do.

Honesty: Treat your company's money as you would your own. Honesty is the best policy. Don't even steal company pens. If anyone notices those pens in your home, they will assume you are untrustworthy. They will assume that the person who steals an egg will also steal the chicken.

Technology: On your first job, be careful to use technology appropriately. Follow the lead of others. Don't be the only one taking notes on your laptop during a business meeting. Don't listen to music on your iPod unless others doing similar work are doing so. Be very careful about what you post on social media. Often, it is easy to post, impossible to remove.

A Chicago attorney told the judge that she needed a postponement of a trial because her father died and she had to attend the funeral in Boston. The judge later discovered on Facebook that she had posted a picture of herself drinking beer at a Chicago sports bar on the original trial date. Her license to practice law was suspended!

Expressing the stupidity of your boss verbally to a coworker is far safer, though still risky, than posting it online where the entire world (including your boss) can see it. Being vitriolic online can even have adverse legal consequences.

Example: Sara posted a Facebook message expressing her hatred of her ex-boyfriend, hoping that someone would kill him. When he was discovered shot to death in a neighboring city, she was arrested and spent several days in jail before being released. Because Sara was unable to prove her whereabouts at the time of the crime, she was subsequently summoned from work several times for additional questioning.

The article in the local newspaper was hardly complimentary. Her current boyfriend suddenly seemed distant, ultimately stopped calling her. Sara's life was in shambles because of a stupid posting, even though she had nothing to do with his death.

The Moral: Before you click SEND, think twice. How can this posting be used to my detriment?

Hiring: Hire people who are smarter than you. The fastest way to climb the corporate ladder is to have good company traveling with you.

Having someone ready to replace you gives you more mobility. Be enthusiastic about the success of others.

Your Next Job: Your first job may not be your first choice of employment, but view it as a learning experience, an opportunity to gain new skills and knowledge about the business world and develop professional contacts.

That first job gives you a chance to network with others in your company, in your field of employment, and in your community. You never know where that next job offer may come from.

Random Advice: When you find a job that is ideal, take it regardless of the pay. If you really have what it takes, your salary will soon reflect your value to the company.

Don't burn bridges. You'd be surprised how many times you have to cross the same river.

Don't work for a company led by someone of questionable character.

Act with courtesy and fairness regardless of how others treat you. Don't let others determine your response.
Don't dismiss a good idea simply because you didn't like the source.

Look for ways to make your boss look good.

Don't expect others to listen to your advice and ignore your example.

Wear a shirt and tie to job interviews even for a job unloading boxcars.

The racehorse which consistently runs just a second faster than other horses is worth millions more. Be willing to give that extra effort that separates the winner from the one in second place.

Work for a company where the expectations of you are high.

Start a "read again file" for articles you might wish to read a second time.

Be happy with what you have while working for what you want.

Be as friendly to the janitor as you are to the chairman of the board. Be especially courteous to secretaries and receptionists; they are the gatekeepers.

Everyday look for some small way to improve the way you do your job.

Seek respect rather than popularity.

Ask yourself if what you are doing today is getting you closer to where you want to be tomorrow.

Remember that winners will do what losers don't want to do. Perform your job better than anyone else can. That is your best job security.

Type out your favorite quotation and place it where you can see it every day. Posting positive affirmations where you can see them each day can help keep you motivated.

Lastly, if you are just starting a new job, re-read this chapter every few days for the first month!

Much of the wisdom in the next chapter, "Starting your own Business," is just as applicable to being a great employee.

***

Starting your own Business

"Who becomes a millionaire? Two-thirds of the millionaires
are self-employed. Usually the wealthy individual owns a
small factory, chain of stores, or a service company."
- Extracted from "The Millionaire Next Door"

Introduction: Perhaps you have considered starting your own business some day because you've wanted to be your own boss, increase your income potential, and achieve your dreams. Perhaps you own a small business that you'd like to expand. While being in business for yourself can be a challenge, it can also provide great personal and financial satisfaction. But starting a business is not something you want to tackle without serious thought and careful planning.

In starting a company you will experience difficulties you never experienced before, but you never know what you are capable of until you try. From early on, we are told what to do by our parents, by our teachers, even by our employers. When starting a business, you are in charge but also on your own. Some have wings to fly, others don't. A major factor in the success of any business is organization and priorities, and that is why several chapters in this book provide extensive coverage of those topics.

Love The Problem: Find a problem and solve it. But don't fall in love with your solution - fall in love with the problem you are trying to solve. Why? Because many times you will find that your solution is not the right one.

139

But by refining your solution, or even changing it entirely, you may be able to establish a successful business. Often, at the onset the right question is more important than what you think is the right answer.

An Example: Around 1895 Donald Jones, a Chicago doctor and inventor, recognized that people were damaging their skeletal structure by walking on cement sidewalks. Foot, knee, hip, and spinal problems were increasing rapidly as the country became more urbanized. In an effort to solve these problems, Donald proposed to cover sidewalks with foam rubber so as to reduce the impact on people's body. He developed extensive equipment to manufacture such coverings, developed proper adhesive to affix the foam rubber to various substances, and spent considerable time trying to convince city officials to buy his solution to this problem. After five years he had not sold a single city on his product. Donald was bankrupt and committed suicide shortly thereafter.

His sister knew that Donald was on to something and convinced her husband, William Mathias Scholl, to reconsider the problem and possible solutions. William was also a doctor and recognized the problem, but his solution was entirely different than Donald's solution.

Instead of lining the sidewalks with rubber foam, his solution was to place the rubber foam inside people's shoes. His solution resulted in a multi-million dollar business and his "solution" is still being sold today. Perhaps you have heard of, or even purchased one of, Dr. Scholl's Shoe Inserts.

The Moral: Fall in love with the problem, and but not necessarily your initial solution! Most successful startups end up doing something different than they originally intended.

The Most Common Reason For Failure: Most new companies die because they didn't make something that people wanted. That is why franchising has become so popular. When you purchase a franchise, you are buying into a business model that has typically worked for many other business owners. Many franchise owners became millionaires by perfecting that business model to their local market. Do your homework before buying a business or franchise.

Don't fall into the image trap: Those are people who enter a business that projects the image they desire; they are more concerned about their image than the numbers. Don't try to impress others unless it impresses your wallet as well.

Think Small At First: When starting a business, you don't have to think too big. Many small ideas evolved into major businesses. McDonald's started with one restaurant, then two. Before long, over a billion hamburgers had been sold. Chances are, you have eaten many of those!

Most successful startup companies have three things in common: (1) They are something the founders want; (2) They are something the founders can build; and (3) They are something that few others realize are worth doing. Sometimes the best ideas seem like bad ideas at the time. Who could build a business out of a website where college students who have no money stare at each other's pictures and comments? From such a stupid business model evolved a company called Facebook!

Take Action: Don't delay acting on a good idea. Chances are, someone else has just thought of it, too. Success will come to the one who acts first. You don't have to be great to start, but you do have to start to be great! Don't let anyone talk you out of pursuing what you believe to be a good idea.

Forget committees. World changing ideas always come from one person acting alone. For example, Mark Zuckerburg (Facebook), Steve Jobs (Apple), and Bill Gates (Microsoft), each left college to start successful companies.

Persistence: Nothing in this world can take the place of persistence. Talent will not. Nothing is more common that unsuccessful men with talent. Genius will not. Unrewarded genius is almost a proverb. Education will not. The world is full of educated derelicts.

Persistence and determination are what is important. A handful of persistence is worth more than a bushel of brains. Or as Thomas Edison put it: Genius is 1% inspiration and 99% perspiration.

Never give up on a dream just because of the length of time that it will take to accomplish it. The time will pass anyway, and often quickly. Sally was questioning the wisdom of starting law school. "I'm already 33; I'll be 36 by the time I graduate." And her father replied, "And how old do you think you will be in three years if you don't go to law school?"

Never give up on what you really want to do. The person with big dreams is more powerful than one with all the facts.

Be Inquisitive: Many think asking a question is a sign of weakness, of inadequacy. Actually, it's a way to learn and grow. Search for the answers to questions that are important to you. Learn to listen to others. There are no stupid questions. Once a month invite someone to lunch who knows more about your business than you do.

Sam Walton, the founder of Walmart, grew his business from a couple of discount stores in Arkansas into the largest retailer in the country by learning from others.

He frequently visited with executives of his future competitors to ask questions. These executives were always willing to demonstrate how knowledgeable they were to this country bumpkin who showed up in his pickup truck wearing his bib overalls.

Many of those future competitors (Kmart, WoolCo, etc.) were eventually driven into bankruptcy by the success of Walmart. There are two obvious lessons to be learned from this story: First, ask others who may know more than you do. Listen closely to their advice. Second, when asked about your own success, give advice sparingly. Don't give away trade secrets. Speak only in generalities.

General Advice: The purpose of this chapter was to encourage you to consider starting your own business, not to give you specific advice on any specific business. While it is tempting to offer specific advice on developing a business plan, marketing, advertising, pricing, selecting a location for your business, and the like, it is almost impossible to offer specific advice of any value without knowing the type of business you plan to start.

The internet is a great source to research the problems and opportunities that face any business you are considering. Professional and trade organizations are another source of specific information that may be helpful.

A Few Random Thoughts: But what I will offer are a few random thoughts about starting or running a business:

Avoid people who belittle your ambitions. Small people always do that. Really great people make you feel that you too can become great. (Mark Twain.)

Success is the ability to go from one failure to another without losing enthusiasm. (Winston Churchill.)

"I have not failed; I have just discovered 10,000 ways that don't work." - A quote from Thomas Edison prior to his discovery of the tungsten filament for his light bulb.

Don't do business with anyone who has a history of suing people. Avoid any lawsuit like the plague; it will drain you emotionally as well as financially. Use lawyers for legal advice, not for business advice. Lawyers are trained to find problems, not solutions.

When facing a difficult task, act as though it is impossible to fail. If you are going after Moby Dick, take along the tartar sauce.

Remember that overnight success usually takes about fifteen years. (Ray Charles)

Keep overhead low and expectations high.

If you reach for the stars and fail, at least you won't end up with a hand full of dirt.

Seek opportunity, not security. A boat in a harbor is safe, but that is not what boats are made for.

Mind the store. No one cares more about your business than you do.

When you are unsure of what to pay someone, ask, "What do you think is fair?" You'll almost always get a reasonable answer.

Don't think that expensive equipment will make up for lack of talent or practice.

Choose a business partner the same way you would chose a tennis partner. Select someone who is strong where you are weak.

Don't worry too much about having insufficient capital. Limited funds are often a blessing, not a curse. Nothing encourages creative thinking and frugality in quite the same way.

Think twice before deciding not to charge for your work. People often don't value what they don't pay for.

Conclusion: My goal was to give you some ideas to think about, to help you formulate your own plan of success. Absorb the ideas you think worthy; discard the rest.

Once your business has turned the corner and becomes profitable , you will have something else to worry about: Taxes! - And that is the topic of our next chapter.

***

A Word about Taxes

*"Taxes and death are one certainty in life. But at least death
doesn't get worse every time Congress meets!"*
- Will Rogers

Taxes are the price we pay for civilization. Laws keep others from
stealing your property; taxes are what fund the enforcement of those
laws. Laws and taxes are necessary in the creation and preservation of
capital. Even though taxes pose a challenge to gaining wealth, we
must accept them as the price we pay for all we have.

The Deficit: What are we to make of the current tax situation and
federal deficit? Won't these heavy and multiple taxes ruin the
country? How will we ever be able to pay off the national debt?
Taxes and public debt have been with us even before America
declared her independence. Neither is going away; both are likely to
become more burdensome in the future. The more you know about
taxes and how they are levied, the greater your ability to legally
minimize them.

Tax Tables: Few tax discussions can begin without at least some
review of the federal income tax tables. Tax tables are essentially
used to calculate how much income tax will be assessed on any given
income and tax status.

Although the government has separate tax tables for "unmarried head
of household" and "Married filing separately", we are limiting our
review to just the "Single" and Married filing jointly" tables and have
included those tables on the following page.

2018 Tax Table for a Single Person

Taxable Income	Tax Rate
$0 – $9,525	10% of taxable income
$9,526 – $38,700	$952.50 *plus* 12% of the amount over $9,525
$38,701 – $82,500	$4,453.50 *plus* 22% of the amount over $38,700
$82,501 – $157,500	$14,089.50 *plus* 24% of the amount over $82,500
$157,501 – $200,000	$32,089.50 *plus* 32% of the amount over $157,500
$200,001 – $500,000	$45,689.50 *plus* 35% of the amount over $200,000
$500,001 or more	$150,689.50 *plus* 37% of the amount over $500,000

2018 Tax Table for Married Couples Filing Jointly

Taxable Income	Tax Rate
$0 – $19,050	10% of taxable income
$19,051 – $77,400	$1,905 *plus* 12% of the amount over $19,050
$77,401 – $165,000	$8,907 *plus* 22% of the amount over $77,400
$165,001 – $315,000	$28,179 *plus* 24% of the amount over $165,000
$315,001 – $400,000	$64,179 *plus* 32% of the amount over $315,000
$400,001 – $600,000	$91,379 *plus* 35% of the amount over $400,000
$600,001 or more	$161,379 *plus* 37% of the amount over $600,000

The Standard Deduction: Taxpayers have the choice of itemizing deductions or taking what is referred to as the Standard Deduction. The standard deduction was increased in 2018 to $12,000 for a single person and $24,000 for a married couple filing a joint return.

That same 2018 legislation that essentially doubles the standard deductions also removed or limited many other possible deductions and exemptions, the result of which is that most middle class taxpayers will be taking the standard deduction than itemizing.

Tax Calculation: Sara, a single person, has earnings of $60,000. Assuming she had no other deductions and took the standard deduction of $12,000, her taxable income would be $48,000. Her income tax liability pursuant to the above table would be $9,140.

In addition, her employer withheld payroll taxes (Social Security and Medicare) of 7.65%, or $4,590, from her paycheck, for a total federal tax of 13,730.

If Sara were self-employed, she would also be liable for what would be the employer's share of payroll taxes, or another $4,590, for total federal taxes of $18,320. In addition, Sara may be subject to state income tax depending of where she lives of perhaps $2,400 (5% of $48,000), for a total tax of $20,720, and a total tax burden is over 1/3 of her earnings. The numbers are almost identical for a married couple with double Sara's income.

If taxpayers had to write a check for this amount at the end of the year, there would be a taxpayer revolt. Fortunately (for the government, but not for Sara), Sara's employer is required to withhold a pro rata portion of this estimated tax burden from each of Sara's paychecks. By paying the tax in small chunks, it does not seem as burdensome.

Income Tax Withholding: The Federal income tax is based on a "pay-as-you-go" system. There are two ways to pay as you go: withholding tax or estimated tax. If you work at a job, your employer most likely withholds income tax from your paychecks. The tax withheld is sent to the IRS on your behalf, and the funds are applied to your Social Security, Medicare, and income taxes for the year.

The amount withheld in each category is reported on your Form W-2 (Wage and Tax Statement), which you receive from your employer shortly after the end of each calendar year. The amount withheld is merely an estimate of what the government thinks will be your final tax bill and is based upon how much you earn, your marital status, and other information you give your employer on Form W-4 (Employee's Withholding Allowance Certificate).

Payroll Tax Withholding: Social Security tax and Medicare tax are also withheld by your employer and have fixed rates. The Social Security tax rate is 6.2% for the employer and 6.2% for the employee (12.4% total). The Social Security tax has a wage base limit of $128,700 for 2018. This means that most employees are required to pay 6.2% Social Security tax on the first $128,700 of their wages.

The Medicare tax rate is currently 1.45% for the employer and 1.45% for the employee (2.9% total). In general, an employee must pay 1.45% Medicare tax on the first $200,000 of their wages.

Self-Employed: If you are self-employed, retired, or have other forms of income, you may be required to pay estimated taxes quarterly. The amount to be paid includes the income tax, and the full Social Security and Medicare tax that would otherwise be paid by both employer and employee. Thus, the self-employed person pays 15.3% on the first $128,700 of earned income.

Withholding Too Much or Too Little: Remember, withholding and estimated tax payments are just that, merely estimates. When you complete your income tax return, you get credit for what you have already paid.

If you have too much tax withheld from your pay during the year, you will receive the overpayment as a tax refund after you file your return. But if you withhold too little, you may have to make estimated payments or be subject to an underpayment penalty.

If you don't pay enough tax, either through withholding or estimated tax payments, you may be subject to both a penalty and interest for underpayment if your total payments (from withholding and estimated tax) do not equal at least 90% of your tax liability for the year, or 100% of your prior year tax, whichever is less.

State income Tax: In addition to the federal government, most states (and even some cities) levy an income tax on their residents. Each has their own formula of what they tax and at what rates, but for those that do have an income tax, the average is about 5%, but may vary greatly depending on the state and the amount of income.

Additional taxes: Even after you pay your federal and state income tax and employment taxes, when you spend what you have left, there are usually additional taxes, such as sales tax (frequently 7% to 9%) on purchasers in most states, annual property taxes on real estate including your home (frequently at 1% to 2% of the fair market value), and additional taxes on specific items, such as automobiles, alcohol and tobacco products.

Marginal Tax Brackets: The concept of the marginal tax brackets is that for each additional dollar that you earn, how much (or what percentage) will go to taxes. As we have seen from the tax table, for the single person earning approximately $60,000, an additional $1,000 would be taxed at 22% (income tax), 7.65% (payroll tax-or 15.3% if self-employed), and perhaps 5% state income tax. Thus, the marginal tax is over 34%, or over 42% for a self-employed taxpayer.

That means if Sara earned an additional $1,000, $340 would go for taxes, or $420 if she were self-employed. Then when Sara spends what is left, other taxes, such as sales tax, will also be paid.   That is why many commentators feel that the marginal tax bracket for most middle class taxpayers might well be close 40% for the employed and 50% for the self-employed. And this is after the 2018 tax act that reduced Sara's marginal income tax bracket from 25% down to 22%.

These high marginal rates encourage taxpayers to find ways to shelter income or even avoid paying taxes on it currently. Contributing to an IRA or a 401(k) plan reduces current income with the hope such funds will be taxed at lower rates when the taxpayer retires.

High marginal rates also encourage people to cheat on their income tax returns by not reporting some income or claiming unsupported deductions.

Tax Avoidance vs. Tax Evasion: Tax avoidance is legally reducing your taxes. Tax evasion is illegally avoiding the payment of taxes. Tax AVOIDANCE is legally reducing your taxes. Tax EVASION is illegally avoiding the payment of taxes. Tax evasion can be not only detrimental to wealth accumulation, but can be detrimental to your liberty as well. Jails are filled with persons who have evaded taxes. Not only do tax evaders have to pay what they previously should have paid in taxes, but they are also assessed penalties and interest. They were guilty of tax evasion, illegally not paying taxes.

Nevertheless tax avoidance can be helpful in accumulating wealth. In many ways Congress has not only allowed us to reduce our tax bill, but has encouraged us to do. Why? Because the activity that generates a tax deduction is often deemed by Congress to be a socially desirable activity.

Congress wants to encourage people to own their own home so it gives homeowners many tax breaks. That is why home mortgage interest is deductible, but rent payments are not.

There are also many tax breaks for owners of rental properties, including depreciation, deduction of expenses, and lower capital gains treatment of gain on sale. Do not hesitate to take legitimate tax deductions and other advantages of the tax laws.

Is All Income Taxed The Same? No, certain categories of income are taxed differently. It is only earned income that is subject to payroll taxes. Interest, dividends, rents, royalties, and capital gains are not.

Municipal Interest: Interest on obligations issued by the states and municipalities are generally not subject to federal income tax. As a result, those interest rates tend to be considerably less than the interest rates of taxable obligations, and thus are advantageous only to taxpayers in the highest tax brackets.

Capital Gains: A capital asset is basically anything that you own or use for personal or investment purposes. This can include stocks, bonds, home furnishings, and the home itself. When you sell a capital asset, the difference between your 'basis' (usually the amount you paid for it) and what you sell it for is called a capital gain or loss.

Capital gains are taxed at regular income tax rates if held for one year or less, but are taxed at more favorable rates if held for more than one year. Currently, the federal long term capital gain tax rate is 0% on the first $38,600 for the single taxpayer, and $77,200 for married taxpayers filing a joint return. The excess, up to 425,800 single and $479,000 married is taxed at 15%. Dividends paid by most stocks and mutual funds are "qualified dividends" and are taxed similar to long term capital gains.

Capital gains and qualified dividends realized inside of an IRA or qualified plan, such as a 401(k) plan, are not taxed when sold, but are taxed as ordinary income when withdrawn from the plan, and subject to possible penalties if the taxpayer is under 59 1/2 years of age.

Appreciation on Assets: The gain – or appreciation in value – on assets is not taxed until the asset is sold. Thus, if the value of your home increases each year, you are not taxed on that appreciation until the home is sold. Thus, long term investments in real estate or common stocks have the advantage that because the gain is not currently taxed, that gain continues to earn additional appreciation for the taxpayer. This concept was discussed in more detail in the chapter on "The Mathematics of Wealth Creation."

Principal Residence: Your home is afforded special tax treatment under the Internal Revenue Code. Not only is the taxable gain subject to capital gain rates, but you can exempt up to $250,000 ($500,000 if married filing a joint return) of gain if you meet the basic requirement of owning and residing in the home for two of the five years prior to sale. You don't have to own it for five years and your occupancy does not have to be continuous.

For example, John has owned his home four years, but had moved to a new home a year before selling it. Because he owned the home for at least two of the five years before sale, and occupied it for two of the five years before sale, he is eligible for the exemption.

This 2-out-of-5 year rule may be used to exclude your capital gains each time you sell or exchange your main home and typically, you can claim the exclusion only once every two years.

Depreciation: Depreciation is an annual income tax deduction that allows you to recover the cost or other basis of certain property over time as you use the property. It is an allowance for the wear and tear, deterioration, or obsolescence of the property. This deduction is allowed even though the property itself may be increasing in value.

Example: Susan purchased a rental home for $200,000. She estimated that the land was worth $40,000 and the improvements (the home itself) worth $180,000. Land cannot be depreciated, but Susan is allowed to claim a depreciation deduction on the building. The IRS requires that a rental home be depreciated over 27 ½ years. So every year Susan can take a depreciation deduction of $6,545 until the improvements are fully depreciated. That deduction can reduce the taxable income she might otherwise have from the rental, and if there is a loss, she may be able to deduct the loss from her other income.

During the first ten years, Susan has been able to deduct $65,450 from her taxable income even though the value of the property has increased 50% in value (5% per year). Susan is entitled to the full depreciation deduction regardless of whether she paid cash or purchased the property with a mortgage.

Depreciation does reduce her basis (or cost) of the asset and upon sale may trigger greater capital gains tax, but still at no greater rate than 25% on the depreciation already claimed and possibly less.

If Susan moves into the rental home and lives there for two years, she can exclude the gain up to $250,000 (single) on sale, but the depreciation already taken may still be taxed at capital gain tax rates.

Step Up In Basis: Capital assets inherited from a decedent generally have a basis adjustment to value on date of death. Susan dies and leaves the rental home to her daughter. The value on Susan's death is $300,000. The daughter subsequently sells the home for $320,000. Only $20,000 is taxed as a capital gain and there is no recapture of depreciation taken by Susan. If the daughter lived in the house for two years following Susan death, she could also use her $250,000 exemption to exclude the gain from taxation.

But It's Deductible: I point out how great our taxes are not so much to scare you but to motivate you to learn more about how income taxes are calculated. Some people tend to buy something because it is tax deductible. Yes, the fact that it is tax deductible may reduce its ultimate cost, but not by as much as you think.

If you buy a $1,000 computer for your business, it is tax-deductible, but if you are in a 22% tax bracket, your savings due to its deductibility is only $220. So the computer's actual cost is $780 - after tax!

While deductibility may enter into your decision to purchase the computer, consider how that $1,000 (or $750 after tax) could be spent or not spent, but invested.

Resources: Lasser's annual tax guide is an excellent source of tax advice. It is available at most bookstores (and Amazon.com) and costs less than $20 (or free at your local library!) It provides an excellent reference guide on what is deductible and what is not.

Even the government publications of tax issues (irs.gov) are well written and helpful in understanding the tax code. Rather than reprinting portions of them here, let me refer you to four relevant publications:

Publication 527 discusses the reporting of rental income, rental expenses, calculating depreciation, and discusses the limitations on deducting passive losses against other income, all in less than fourteen pages. Of interest to any homeowner are Publication 530- Tax Information for Homeowners and Publication 523- Selling your Home.

Lastly, Instructions for Schedule D-Capital Gains and Losses should be of interest to most any investor.

Do It Yourself? Consider completing your own income tax return at least once, so you can get a better sense of how income, deductions, and taxes work. After you have completed your own return, you may still wish to have a tax preparer review your return.

Computer Programs: TurboTax or other computer tax programs are available at most of the office supply stores. TurboTax will, if you desire, prompt you for possible deductions you may have forgotten or be unaware of.

Such programs are not only useful for preparing your tax return, but can also serve as analytical tool for evaluating different situations.

After you have printed out or filed your return, you can go back and test different scenarios, such as calculating your additional tax liability if you earned an additional $1,000, or how much less tax liability if you had an additional $1,000 in rental expenses.

I once used TurboTax to determine if it would be better to sell two rental properties in 2007 rather than one in 2007 and one in 2008. I had sold one property earlier in the year and had another property under contract with a developer near the end of the year. The purchaser didn't care if we closed at the end of December or early January.

By using TurboTax, I was able to save over $10,000 in taxes. I don't want to give you the answer, because it might be different for your situation. Moreover, the answer may be different now that what was back then. But there is no substitute for actually running the numbers. TurboTax can run these very complex and interrelated calculations for you in less than a second!

That's it for taxes for now. We will revisit the topic in the chapters on Real Estate Investing. Next we will discuss what millionaires actually own.

***

What Do Millionaires Actually Own?

"I'd give a thousand bucks to be one of them millionaires!"
- Will Rogers

The Millionaire Next Door: Wouldn't it be nice if we could see what millionaires own? Perhaps that would be an indication of how they became wealthy. A book was written several years ago that attempted to do just that. The Millionaire Next Door, written by Thomas J. Stanley and William D. Danko, described the three major means by which millionaires were able to accumulate their wealth, which were:

- Own real estate
- Own your own business
- Work in corporate management.

This book is strongly recommended to anyone interested in becoming a millionaire.

IRS Statistics: Ever wonder what investments and other assets the "average" millionaire owns? Interestingly, an Internal Revenue Service web site summarized the various categories of assets owned by persons who filed federal Estate Tax Returns in 2011. A federal estate tax return (IRS Form 706) is required to be filed by the executor of any person dying with assets above a statutory amount. That return is due within nine months after the date of death.

Here is an analysis of those filings for all persons with estates between $5 million and $10 million ($ in thousands):

Primary Residences	$ 1,132,431	8.2%
Other Real Estate & Farm	2,784,662	20.1%
Closely Held Businesses	778,505	5.6%
Public Stocks, Mutual Funds	2,814,645	20.3%
Bonds-Fed,State, & Corp.	1,856,567	13.4%
Cash, MM, CD's, etc.	1,499,576	10.8%
Life Insurance-Death Benefit	424,614	3.0%
IRA & other Retirement Plans	1,332,368	9.6%
Mortgages, Promissory notes	326,476	2.3%
Other (Collectibles, etc.)	925,139	6.7%
Total	$13,874,974	100.0%

The average value of the primary residence owned by these "millionaires" who declared a primary residence was only $756,973, but that did constitute over 8% of their net worth. Qualified plans, such as Individual Retirement Accounts (IRAs), 401(k), and 403(b) plans, represented over 9% of their net worth.

These estates reported almost 30% in real estate (residences and other real estate) and 33% in publicly traded securities (stocks, bonds, and mutual funds). 10% was invested in cash and equivalents, and only 6% in closely held businesses.

But Consider Age: Keep in mind that the average age for the decedent who filed an estate tax return in 2011 was approximately 78 years of age. Many people who perhaps gained their wealth through ownership of a small business or through rental real estate very likely sold such assets upon retiring and long before they died. People in their 70's rarely buy rental real estate or start new businesses.

Some people even sell their homes in their later years if they have to move into assisted living or a nursing home. Therefore it is highly likely that the percentages of assets in closely-held business and real estate for these same persons ten or twenty years earlier were considerably higher than those shown above.

Conclusions: So what does this information tell the inspiring millionaire?

1. The "forced savings" in IRAs and qualified plans can be an important building block to wealth.

2. Even for retired wealthy persons, ownership in a privately held business may constitute a significant portion of their wealth. The actual number of persons holding an interest in such companies was only one-tenth of those owning real estate, and therefore, for those deceased taxpayers who actually did own an interest in private companies, the percentage of their estate represented by private companies is likely much greater than the 5% shown above.

3. Real estate is probably the most important sector of wealth, but may be on par with publicly-traded securities, such as stocks, mutual funds, and bonds.

4. A primary residence was perhaps an important building block in obtaining wealth. That concept will be explored in later chapters in this book.

5.

No Specific Advice In Some Areas: Although this book does not offer you specific advice about starting a business, we do, however, point out the advantages of starting your own business. The motivation, initiative, and ideas must come from you.

This book does not help you become a corporate executive, but we can point out the advantages of being one. Proper education, including advanced degrees such as an M.B.A., law degree, or engineering degree, can certainly be helpful.

Specific Advice in Other Areas: This book DOES, however, offer the reader very specific advice on investing in the stock market in the following two chapters.

This book DOES offer the reader more specific advice on buying a home and investing in small rental properties, and has done so in three of the following chapters.

So let's get started on investing and learn how to outperform (have greater returns - make more money!) most individual investors.

***

Stock Market Investment - Diversification

"I am more concerned about the return OF my capital,
than I am about the return ON my capital!
- Will Rogers

"The recent market crash doesn't bother me, as I have
all of my money safely invested in collectible plates!"
- Ellen DeGeneres

Why Stocks: The stock market offers considerable risks as well as considerable rewards. Over almost any ten year period, the rate of return on investments in stocks has generally been several percentage points greater than the return on bonds, savings accounts, or certificates of deposit.

Rate Of Return: Return, or rate of return, is a term used to measure the annual percentage by which an investment increases in value over a period of time, typically one year, and includes any interest, dividends, and the increase or decrease in the actual value of the investment.

For instance, a savings account that pays 2% per year would have a return of 2%; a stock that pays a 1% dividend, but which also increases in value by 9% during the year, has a 10% annual return.

Stock Picking: It is tempting to write a treatise on how in invest in the stock market, describing price/earnings ratios, dividend and earnings yields, contrary investing , technical analysis (charting) and the like. If you want to learn more about those topics, you are welcome to read many of the literally millions of books and newsletters available on the subject.

Most of these books and newsletters won't help you much, although they will make you feel more confident as you make mediocre investment decisions. The next chapter offers the reason for this cynicism.

Diversification: There are, however, a few investment topics worth discussing for the novice investor. The first of those is importance of diversification. Novice investors often think that wise investing means finding the "best investment" (the best stock to buy) and putting all of your money into that one investment. Why would you invest in a stock that you think might not increase in value as much as your first choice? Such a strategy would be great if you were always right, but no investor, not even Warren Buffett (the Oracle of Omaha, and perhaps the world's greatest investor) is right all the time. Most experienced investors just hope to be right more than 50% of the time.

Although many investors or financial advisors claim to be gurus when it comes to investing in the stock market, nobody knows for sure whether any one stock will increase in value during the next day, week, month, or even year. Yes, some investors get lucky one year, but then suffer losses the next.

Losses: Only experienced investors realize that losses are more significant than gains. Therefore, preventing major losses should be given greater priority than realizing greater gains. Why is that?

Let's say you invest $1,000. If in the first year you experience a 50% loss, the value of your investment would be $500. The next year you would need a 100% gain to offset that loss. If you had only a 50% gain, that $500 would increase in value by only $250 (50% x 500 = 250) to $750. It would take a doubling of your $500 to get back to $1,000, and that is a 100% gain.

An Example: To demonstrate the importance of diversification when it comes to investing, let's look as two investors who over time invest in four stocks that had a combined return of 2.5%. Investor A invests his $4,000 by buying an equal amount of all four stocks at the beginning of period. As you can see below, his profit is $100 (2.5% of $4,000.)

Investment:	Return	Profit/Loss
Stock A	+50%	+$500
Stock B	-30%	-$300
Stock C	+40%	+$400
Stock D	-50%	-$500
Total PROFIT:		+$100
Ending Value		$4,100

Investor B, on the other hand, invested his $4,000 in only one stock at a time:

Investment:	Return:	Change in Value	Account Value in Investor B
Stock A	+50%	+ $2,000	$6,000
Stock B	-30%	- $1,800	$4,200
Stock C	+40%	+ $1,680	$5,880
Stock D	-50%	- $2,940	$2,940

Balance in Investor B's account: $2,940, for a total LOSS of $1,060!

Ah, you might be saying, that's because he had the large loss at the end of the period. But if you reverse the order of the stocks, you will find that regardless of the order in which he invested, the end value is the same, and that is $2,940. To summarize: Investor A gained $100 while Investor B lost $1,060! This example is perhaps the simplest way to demonstrate the importance of diversification.

Mutual Funds: Mutual Funds are investments offered by a great many sponsors to the public. They are highly regulated by the Securities and Exchange Commission, a branch of the federal government. In that regard, such funds are reasonably safe from the standpoint of management theft, securities manipulation, and other causes of losses when you invest in individual companies, and especially in "private investments."

Mutual funds allow small investors to participate in a diversified portfolio of securities. For the investor with, say, $1,000, the commission and other costs of purchasing shares in even 20 different companies would be prohibitive. That same investor can invest indirectly in one hundred or more stocks by investing in a mutual fund.

Load Funds vs. No-Load Funds: There are "load" mutual funds and "no-load" mutual funds. Load funds charge an upfront commission, usually paid to the person or firm who sold you the fund. If you take the initiative, you can easily identify no-load funds with the same investment goals and similar past performance as most if not all load funds.

As someone succinctly put it, "Paying a commission to a salesman does not enhance the investment performance of the fund. It merely reduces your dollars invested in the fund, which, other things being equal, results in a lower return on your investment."

When an investor buys and sells a typical no-load mutual fund, there is no commission. If you bought yesterday, and sold today, and there was no change in the underlying value of the fund's securities, you would have neither a gain nor a loss. So such purchasers are very appropriate for the small investor.

Within any mutual fund, the management charges a fee, which, depending on the fund, may range between as low as 0.1% to well over 2% per year. Obviously, the greater the fee, the more the fund has to earn to deliver the same net return to the investor. Some funds, such as international funds specializing in growth opportunities require more research, and more expense, in selecting the stocks in which it will invest.

Ones that merely mirror an index, such as the S&P 500 index funds described in the next chapter, do not have highly-paid analysts to select stocks, but merely select the stocks upon which the index is based.

Issuers: Shares of mutual funds are typically purchased directly from the issuer, and when sold, are sold back to the issuer. Fidelity, Vanguard, and Charles Schwab are just a few of the many issuers of mutual funds.

ETFs: Exchange Traded Funds, sometimes abbreviated to "ETFs", are similar to mutual funds in that you are investing in a basket of securities. But EFTs are bought and sold on exchanges like stocks.

 And thus, depending on supply and demand, may sell at a price that is greater than or less than the value of the underlying securities. Also, there is typically a commission both when buying and when selling an ETF.

Because ETF's typically have lower internal management fees, larger investors may find them more profitable as the lower management fee may more than offset the commission when buying and selling such investments, especially if you are a buy-and-hold investor.

And this background leads us into our next chapter on foolproof investing!

***

The Foolproof Method of Investing!

"I invest only when the market is going up and I sell when it goes down." Quote by a confused investor who does not understand why he is constantly losing money when investing.

Study after study has shown that the average individual investor earns considerably less than the "market." One reasonable measure of the "market" is the Standard and Poor 500, which is an index of the stock prices of the 500 largest publicly-traded companies in the U.S. That index is often referred to as the "S&P 500." Although it only represents, perhaps, 10% of the publicly traded stocks in the U.S., because the index includes the largest companies, and is weighted by total market value of each, it probably represents over 80% of the value of the total market of publicly-traded common stocks in the U.S. Thus, that index represents is a good measure of the change in value of the stock market. Here is a 30 year chart of that index:

In addition to the changes in the value of the index, it should be noted that the index on average also has had a 2% dividend rate.

Nobody can invest directly in the index. The index is merely a figure calculated by a financial publishing company named "Standard and Poor." In publishing this daily figure, the company uses complex calculations and not just the daily closing price on each of the 500 securities that is part of that calculation. There are, however, a number of mutual funds and exchange traded funds that attempt to mimic the S&P 500 by owning those same securities and in the same proportions.

Investor Returns: The individual investor studies, conducted by some of the largest brokerage firms in the country, noted that, for example, if the S&P 500 increased by 10% per annum during a given period, the individual investor's return was only about 5% per annum.

Why is this? And how can you beat the returns of most individual investors and even most mutual funds? And without spending a lot of time analyzing companies? There is a simple method of doing so, which will be explained later in this chapter.

Individual Investors Underperform the Market: There are a great many reasons why the average individual investor grossly under performs the market. The reason offered most frequently, and probably the most important, is that the individual investor tends to purchase after the market has risen substantially, and then to sell after the market has fallen.

In effect, he is doing exactly the opposite of what his goal should be. Instead of buying low and selling high, most individual investors act emotionally and end up buying high and selling low.

As one financial planner observed, "When there is a sale on stocks, nobody wants to buy, but when prices have increased, everybody wants in!"

But in reality there are many other factors that tend to work against the individual investor. Let's explore some of those.

Fees: John Bogle (Vanguard Funds) is famous for creating the first "S&P 500 Fund." His theory was that costs and expenses do matter. To the extent you can minimize such costs, your return will be greater.

The average investor who uses a financial planner is typically paying an annual fee of 1% or more. Truly great financial planners have their place in helping clients ride out market cycles, in helping clients to stay diversified, and avoiding many of the "bad investments" out there, and providing other valuable financial and planning advice.

Nevertheless, many who masquerade as financial planners do so merely to sell high commission investments that often don't work out well for their clients. A mediocre financial planner can do more harm than good. But regardless, the 1% advisor fee does represent a significant reduction in your return. If your financial planner charges 1% and is investing your money in a no-load mutual fund with a management fee of 1%, you have just lost about 2% of your potential market return when compared with investing directly in an S&P 500 fund. Fees matter!

Because mutual funds and exchange traded fund own a high percentage of the value of publicly-traded stocks, they cannot, in total, outperform the market. In essence, they ARE the market, and with management fees, commissions, expenses, and the like, it would be impossible for them, on average, to outperform, or even match, the market.

Believing That Performance Will Continue: Yes, some mutual funds over a given period of time will do better than the market and some will do worse. It has been shown that the funds that do better in a given year more often than not do worse in the following year. Usually the ones that do better happen to concentrate their investments in industries that just happened to do better that year. The Securities and Exchange Commission requires mutual fund prospectuses to state, in essence, that past performance is no guarantee of future results.

That is worth repeating: Past performance is no guarantee of future results. Few individual investors believe this, which is one of the reasons why individual investors tend to underperform the market. It's easier for an investment advisor to recommend a mutual fund that had stellar performance last year or two over one that had mediocre performance. Once again, we see the individual investor "buying high."

Commissions: There are also commissions when an investor buys and sells securities. They may range between a few dollars per transaction to as much as 1%. Discount brokers, such as Fidelity, Vanguard, Charles Schwab, and others, typically charge a flat $4 to $8 per transaction, almost regardless of the number of shares.

"Full service brokerage firms," such as Merrill Lynch, Morgan Stanley, and UBS usually charge many times as much. For example, the commission on a $60,000 sale of stock issued by a major company might cost only, say, $5 at a discount broker, but may cost $600 or more at a "full service" broker.

Commissions are often negotiable, but, of course, many brokers don't want to advertise that, as the broker frequently receives a percentage of those commissions.

To the extent the average individual investor uses a full service broker, and trades stock several times per year, the average investor's return will be reduced by, perhaps, another 1% or more.

Excessive Turnover: If the broker receives a portion of the commission, can you see why the broker always has a "hot deal?" The broker is trying to convince you to sell what you now own and purchase a different security. Two commissions! Discount brokers typically do not compensate their employees based on transactions.

Slippage: Slippage is the term investment professionals use for the difference between the price you pay to purchase a security and the price you would get if you sold the security at the same point in time. It is the spread between the "bid and ask" prices. The Ask Price is generally what you would pay if you bought "at the market price" and the Bid Price is the price you would receive if you sold "at the market price."

The bid and ask prices of large, high volume stocks are often only a few pennies difference, such as Bid-$24.06 Ask-24.08. In more thinly traded securities, the spread between the bid and ask may be much greater, such as Bid-$24.06 Ask-$24.30.

But you may say, but that's only 24 cents, what's the big deal? Realize that 24 cents is approximately 1% of the purchase price. For the individual investor, there goes another 1% or so of his or her return.

Investor Expenses: There are numerous newsletters, tools, and software available to help an investor determine what to buy and when. Most do help a person make money - the person selling the system! Such expenses add to the expense of investing, and thus reduce the ultimate return.

Many of these newsletters and systems will get you into "volatile" stocks - stocks which increase far more than average when the market goes up, but fall even faster when the market declines.

Excessive Trading: Perhaps you have heard of "day traders" - investors who generally buy and sell a stock within the same day or within a few days, hoping to make a small gain on each transaction. Day traders often use "sophisticated software" and other tools to help them determine what and when to buy and sell.

It has been shown that over 90% of the day traders have lost money - often a very significant portion of their investments. And as one commentator has suggested, "it's just a matter of time before the other 10% lose their money as well."

Frequent trading also results in gains being taxed each year and at ordinary rates, unless the security has been held for over one year. Mathematically, it can be shown that an investor is better off with an 8% annual return sold at the end of 15 years than a 9.25% return taxed each year at ordinary rates. That is one of the reasons why we recommend a buy and hold strategy.

Furthermore, an investor is better off with a 7.25% return at the end of the 15th year if the increase in value is not taxed at all. As discussed earlier, the gain on the sale of a primary residence can generally be avoided under current tax law.

Because the S&P 500 funds mimic the index, and there is very little change from year to year in the stocks making up the index, there is very little tax liability during your holding period. This permits the increase in value to be invested for compound growth until the fund is actually sold.

The Competition: The big New York financial firms have trading software like we do, but they can execute hundreds of transactions while the individual investor is studying just one stock. The big boys have resources the individual investor lacks. The big boys have staff to study industries and the periodic reports of companies. To the extent the big boys earn a greater return than the market - and many of the investment banks do - that means the remaining investors must, on average, earn less.

Insider Trading: Some "insider trading" is illegal, but very few traders actually get caught. Martha Stewart was an exception, as she will readily admit. But what about the employee who knows his company is doing well and has a great future and does NOT sell his stock - or perhaps even buys more.

Not to vilify Bill Gates, but to the extent he held his shares of Microsoft for 20 years and earned a greater return than the market average, does that not leave less return for the remaining investors? How many other corporate executives hold because of good news they hear inside the company or sell in advance of bad news being made public?

The market is comprised largely institutional investors, such as mutual funds, pensions, and other large investors. They, together with individual investors, make up the market. To the extent that one group earns a greater return than the market average, the other group must, by definition, earn a return that is less than the market average.

Does all this sound so negative that the individual investor doesn't stand a chance of earning a decent return? Perhaps, but given that equities (stocks) have returned on average 8% or more per annum during most ten year periods, the individual investor can still earn a fair return even if he earns a percent or two less than the market's return.

A Foolproof Strategy: How would you like an investment strategy which is (1) easy to implement - does not require a lot of time; and (2) is almost guaranteed to do better than 90% of the individual investors, and likely to beat the returns of over 80% of the mutual funds over time?

The investment I am suggesting is a no-load "S&P 500 Fund" offered by any one of the many sponsors, such as Vanguard, Schwab, or Fidelity.

Larger individual investors may want to consider exchange traded funds, which usually have lower internal expenses, even though the investor will incur a brokerage fee when the ETF is bought or sold.

Whatever you have to invest in the stock market, simply invest it into one of these funds and you are almost guaranteed to earn over 99% of the "market return." This system is virtually foolproof, is easy to implement, and is very diversified. It's just not very exciting to discuss with your friends.

Want to play the market a little and buy individual stocks you think will do well? Then place only 90% in the S&P 500 and invest the other 10% stocks you like to talk about. But let me warn you, over time you are likely to wish that you had placed all your funds in the S&P 500 Fund!

An Even Better Investment: Stocks have, on average, had an annualized rate of return of about 8% during most 10 year periods during the past 50 years. Are greater returns available in real estate? For the long term investor, real estate investing, in either your own home or a rental home, or both, may offer even greater profits over time, and is the topic of our last three chapters.

***

Real Estate Investing: Your Home

"Invest in Real Estate - They're not making any more of it!"
- Will Rogers

Home Prices: It seems hard to believe, but the average cost of a home in 1950 was approximately $7,500; in 1960 it was 12,000. It should be noted that the "average home" is considerable larger in size today than it was in 1950.

Although the price of homes has increased dramatically, the rate of increase has not been constant, and in fact, prices did drop significantly between 2007 and 2010. The great recession of 2008-2011 was triggered largely by the decline in housing prices which began the year before. Housing prices reached a peak in the first quarter of 2007 ($255,000) and did not recover until the first quarter of 2013 (258,000). Here is a chart of the average home prices from 1970 through the end of 2017 from the Economic Data division of Federal Reserve Board:

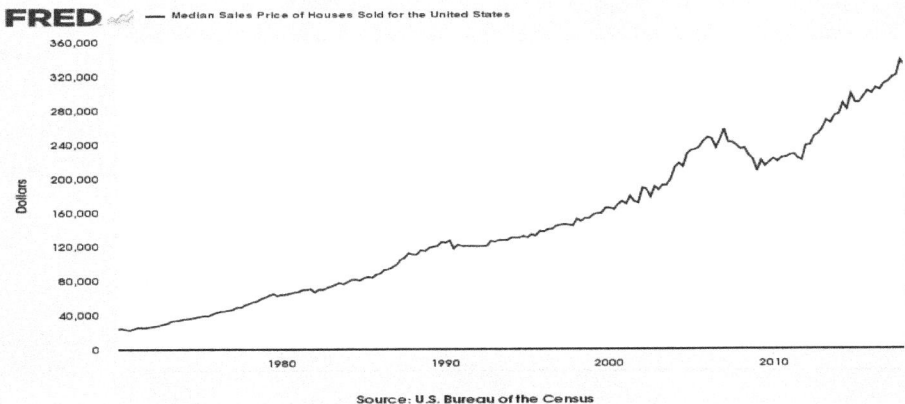

Source: U.S. Bureau of the Census

177

Here is a summary of the data from the above chart:

Year	Average Price	Dollar Change	Annualized % Change
1970	23,000	-	-
1980	64,900	41,900	10.93%
1990	117,000	52,100	6.07%
2000	168,800	51,800	3.73%
2005	236,400	67,600	6.97%
2010	224,100	(12,300)	-1.06%
2015	295,800	71,700	5.71%
2017	337,900	42,400	4.54%

Annualized appreciation rate since 2018 has been 4.44%, and the annualized rate of appreciation since 1970 has been 5.76%.

Yes, there was a four year period during the Great Recession (2008 to 2012) during which the average home price decreased. The housing market peaked around 2005 to 2007, and reached a low around 2010. Nevertheless, the annualized rate of appreciation during the ten year period from 2005 to 2015 was 2.27%. That may have been of little consolation to home owners who bought in 2005 and sold in 2011.

This chart is useful in not only showing the dramatic increase in the average cost of the family home over time, but it also demonstrates that there are variations in that return, including a fairly long period of negative returns. Thus, any investment in a single family home should be viewed as long term commitment.

Although you may be able to make a reasonable profit over a two year period, it is also possible that you could sustain a sizable loss, or even all of your investment. Sadly, many people today are unwilling to make long-term commitments.

If you think it is likely you will move to a different city within the next few years, perhaps the purchase of a home would not be recommended.

Home Ownership: Some people may argue that the cost of home ownership today is not much different than the cost of renting, so why own? While that argument may be true today, that is a very short term view.

Let's say you purchased an "average" home in 2000 for $168,800 with 10% down ($16,880) and borrowed the remainder at 6% amortized over 30 years. Your monthly mortgage payments of principal and interest would be $911, plus an additional amount, say $239, for taxes and insurance, for a total payment of $1,200.

Your identical twin thought you were stupid to buy because he was renting a similar home for only $800. His rent was not deductible, but your interest and property taxes (approximately $900 per month) were, saving you perhaps $270 per month. So your net after tax cost was actually less than $1,000.

Eighteen Years Later: Here we are in early 2018. Your home is now worth over $337,000. Remember our formula for net worth: Assets minus Liabilities = Net Worth. Your mortgage is paid down to $95,000, giving you "equity" in your home of $242,000. Your initial investment of $16,880 has resulted in your equity in your home of $242,000, which is an annualized return of almost 16%!

Furthermore, if the home appreciated at 6% during that first year, its value increased by over $10,000 in 2000. That is over a 50% return during the first year on your down payment of $16,880! That is why we are able to project that your potential earnings on a home may be 12% to 15% over a multi-year holding period.

Some may criticize this analysis for ignoring closing costs when the home was purchased and selling commission if you sold today. Even after allowing for an initial payment of $20,000 and a 6% commission if sold today, the annualized after tax return would be over 14%! And that was in spite of the "Great Recession"!

Your payments are now $1,350 per month with the increase in taxes and insurance. You still have some deductions for income tax purposes, and over $400 per month is going to pay down your mortgage. After the tax savings and the mortgage pay down, your out-of-pocket expense in 2018 is, perhaps, only $800 per month.

Just as home prices have doubled during the past 18 years, so have rents. So, your twin brother's rent is $1,600 now and he has no equity. Furthermore, your twin brother has had to move three times because his landlord decided to sell his house.

So what did your twin brother do with his "savings" during those early years? He probably ended up giving it back, and then some, in the later years for his higher rent and the cost of moving!

In Twelve Years: Twelve years from now your mortgage will be paid off, and that $911 portion of your monthly payment will drop to zero! You can now live in your home for only cost of taxes and insurance – perhaps $500 per month.

The value of your home is likely to increase – let's say at a modest 3% per annum. So in twelve years the fair market value of your home is likely to be $481,700, and with no mortgage, that is all equity. That represents a gain of $312,900 based upon your initial purchase price of $168,800.

Your twin brother's rent is likely to be considerably greater in twelve years, perhaps over $2,200 per month to rent a similar home.

If you sold the home in twelve years, how much income tax might be payable? As you may recall from the chapter on taxation, married couples can exempt up to $500,000 on the sale of a principal residence, so absolutely no tax would be due. A single person has a $250,000 exemption, so only $62,900 would be subject to long term capital gains tax. That tax at 15% would be only $9,435.

Yes, there are other costs and disadvantages to home ownership, but most people who have owned their home for 12 years or more will tell you that the costs are negligible compared to the advantages.

And that, in a nutshell is why purchasing a single family home could be the most profitable investment of your life!

Don't Worry About What Others Say: Jennifer purchased her first home in 2000. She knew her home was pretty small compared to her father's house in Phoenix that he had purchased some 15 years earlier.

When her father came from Phoenix to visit Jennifer thereafter, he asked her how much she had paid. When she told him she had paid $168,800, he told her that that was exactly what he had paid for his house. Then he said, "All things considered, I'd rather live in my house. How could this house ever be worth much more than $168,800? You paid too much!"

Jennifer was smart enough to not argue with her father. Jennifer knew she had paid a fair price. She had looked at over 30 houses in the neighborhood and had made several offers on other homes that were turned down. She had negotiated on this house for over two months. The owner wanted $189,000 and she finally got him to accept $168,800. Jennifer may or may not have gotten a bargain price, but she was sure that she paid a fair price or less for her home.

Jennifer was single when she purchased that first three bedroom home. She rented out two of the bedrooms to friends with whom she worked. She received enough rent to almost cover the monthly mortgage payment, plus all three of them split the phone and utilities! With very little housing expense, she was able to save up enough to buy another couple of rental homes during the next few years.

In 2013 Jennifer applied for and obtained a new mortgage. Not only was it a very favorable interest rate, and was able to obtain $60,000 in cash which she subsequently used to purchase a new home that she moved into. She kept her old home as a rental property.

In 2015 she sold that original home. Her gain (up to $250,000) was exempt from taxation! That is because she met the requirement of owning the property and residing there for two of the five years before sale. Her residency is not required to be the most recent two years.

The moral of this story: Don't worry about what other people think. Think for yourself. Control your own destiny. The road of life is paved with flattened squirrels who couldn't make a decision to act in their own best interest.

Other Real Estate Investments: What about other real estate investments? Let's discuss these other alternatives:

Vacant Land: The most speculative and romantic real estate investment is raw land. Fortunes have been made and many are still being made. The principle sounds simple: Buy land in the path of growth and then wait five to 10 years to resell and cash in the chips.

This might work for you, too, if you can:

1. Afford to set aside $100,000 to $500,000 that pays no income;

2. Afford to pay $3,000 to $15,000 per year in taxes; and

3. Have the good fortune to accurately pick a parcel of land that will be in the path of progress and can be easily re-zoned before you wish to sell.

Land investments are not for everybody. You must have a lot of insight and a lot of money, and often times, a lot of patience, and a lot of luck.

It is difficult to finance vacant land. If you can even find lenders to finance vacant land, they usually want a larger down payment and want to amortize the loan over only five years. And you will pay a higher interest rate than on an owner-occupied home, or even a rental home.

The growth that has been predicted must materialize. Building restrictions, loss of a major employer, or a sudden spike in interest rates could significantly reduce the value of your property. A typical investor would only buy such a property when everything looks rosy, which means he would be paying top dollar.

Commercial Property: Commercial property can be an individual unit or a large, multi-million-dollar project. It's a highly specialized field that takes a lot of capital, carries high risk, and should be left alone by the average investor.

Many commercial properties are often custom built for a specific use. If the tenant ever leaves, it could take many months or ever years to re-rent the property. Moreover, extensive renovations may be required by the new tenant. No doubt you have seen such buildings (like a Pizza Hut or a grocery store) sit empty for a year or more.

With a single family house, you can usually rent it out within a month. If not, you can reduce the rent slightly and rent it out during the second month. There are far more potential renters of a single family home than of an empty Pizza Hut or Taco Bell.

Apartment Properties: Multi-unit investment property can give you the tax shelter and profits similar to what you will find in single family homes. However, apartment properties are management intense and require more capital investment and more knowledge than you can obtain in a short period of time.

It's hard to start out small with a 20 unit apartment building. You can more easily buy single family homes, one at a time as money becomes available.

The risks inherent with multi-family units are sometimes too great for the average investor. A bad plumbing problem, small fire, or rent control can affect all your units in an apartment building; such is usually not the case with multiple single family dwellings. Tenant turnover tends to be much higher in apartments than in single family homes, especially in furnished apartments.

With single family homes you can usually obtain quality tenants who will stay for a long period of time. With apartments you will often be saddled with tenants who will only be with you a short period of time. One bad tenant can affect all of your other tenants; not so in multiple single family home investments.

Another disadvantage of apartments is the method by which they are typically valued. The value is often determined as a function of rents received. Thus the owner must constantly be upgrading the units and raising rents to increase value. Sometimes this is easier said than done.

With single-family homes the value is determined by what similar homes are selling for in the area, or in some growing urban areas, by the value of the land for redevelopment.

For several decades we have been in a long-term inflationary period that will continue to increase the value of your single-family home investment, and will also increase the rent you can collect.

With respect to some smaller homes in good neighborhoods near the downtown of a larger city, the land values have grown to exceed the value of the property in its current use. It is not unusual in many metropolitan areas to see such small houses being "popped up" with new second stories, or even torn down and replaced with a two-story home or even a duplex.

In other words, a buyer may be after the land, and will demolish the house to build a larger home. That rarely happens with apartment buildings, because the value of an apartment building initially tends to be a much greater percentage of the purchase price of the property, than with a single family home.

Rent Controls: Rent control ordinances, although common only in large cities, typically are directed only at apartment buildings and exempt single family dwellings and duplexes. In the long run rent control brings about rental shortages and drives up rents nearby that do not have controls.

The Single Family Home as a Rental Property: In this chapter we discussed the economic advantages of owning your own home. Do the advantages of home ownership apply equally to owning a rental home or how are they different? And what are the additional opportunities and challenges? Those will be the topics discussed in our next chapter.

***

Real Estate Investing: Rental Homes

"Generally speaking, real estate is a bad investment. 90% of all the real estate in this country has not even appreciated at the rate of inflation."

No Appreciation: I grew up in Albuquerque, my in-laws live in Omaha. I drive to both cities a couple of times each year. 95% of the land in between has hardly changed at all in the past thirty years. It's still dry farm or ranch land, some is forest land owned by the federal government, and some is desert.

Horizon Corporation was marketing five acre lots "just 40 miles from Albuquerque" some 50 years ago for only $2,000. Almost no homes were ever built on those lots. Albuquerque today has quadrupled in population since then. That Horizon development is still about 35 miles from the Albuquerque city limits. An owner of such a lot today would have a difficult time selling his lot today for $2,000. As the old saying goes, the three most important things in buying real estate are: Location, Location, and Location.

Where Is The Appreciation? So what has appreciated in value? It's the real estate in or near the major cities. For example, in my region of the country, Denver, Albuquerque, Salt Lake City, Phoenix, and even Omaha have seen both population increases and increases in home prices. But even smaller cities in between, such as Colorado Springs, Pueblo, Kearney, and Lincoln have seen such increases. These are just typical of a great many of the cities in the U.S.

187

Ease of Investment: For the small investor, single family rental homes make the most sense. The down payment is low and the rent can cover all or at least most of the mortgage payment. If a tenant moves out, the property can usually be re-rented in a short period of time, either by fixing up the property or lowering the rent.

In almost any civilized country, if you own your home and the home next to you as a rental, you can survive quite well. Not rich, but you have an almost free place to live plus the income from the rental.

For instance, such a rental may rent for $1,500 per month. That's about the same monthly amount that a typical worker can expect to receive from Social Security. That worker took 35 years of working to obtain the same income that the rental property owner receives each month. The rental income can double your retirement income! If you have 5 rental properties, your income may look like that of a retired senior executive at IBM!

A recent Gallup survey showed that one out of every seven American families own real estate other than their home; and six per cent of American families that owned their own home also owned another single-family residence. That means that over several million Americans own rental homes.

Such ownership confirms the general belief that single family home investments are the surest, fastest, and easiest way to make big money in real estate. It is very common for an investor to earn 9% to 10% or more after tax each year on the money invested in rental homes.

The profit isn't realized, of course, until the property is sold. The profit is not taxed until the property is sold, and when sold, your gain is taxed at favorable long-term capital gains tax rates.

And because you are not taxed until the property is sold, you have more money invested each year than if the gain were taxed as the property appreciates in value.

Differences from Owner Occupied Homes: Many of the economic advantages of the owner-occupied home apply to the ownership of a rental home. Before examining the purchase in the last chapter as a rental home, let's discuss a few of the differences:

1. Purchasing a rental home generally requires a larger down payment and the interest rate tends to be about 1% greater. Both differences tend to reduce your rate of return somewhat, but can be negated if you first purchase an owner-occupied home, then later purchase another home to live in and convert the first home to a rental. Some investors have done this several times and thus always got favorable financing what later became a rental home.

2. The owner of a rental home can take a tax deduction for depreciation. That tax advantage is not available for an owner-occupied home. However, on the sale of the rental home, that depreciation taken is taxed at a rate typically greater than the usual long term capital gain tax rate.

3. The "principal residence exemption" of $250,000 ($500,000 for a married couple filing jointly) is available only on an owner-occupied home meeting certain requirements. The exemption is not available on the sale of a rental home. However, if you own a rental home and then move into it and occupy it as your principal residence for two years, you generally can use the exemption on the gain.

Potential Return: Let's examine how the return on a rental home might differ from an owner-occupied home discussed in the prior chapter.

As you may recall, the purchase price in 2000 was $168,800. The mortgage company is likely to require a 20% down payment, or $33,760. Closing costs might be greater, plus some fixup and vacancy while a tenant is found. So we will use $38,000 as our initial investment.

The mortgage interest rate is likely to be 1% greater than would be charged on an owner occupied home, but because you put 20% down, the principal and interest payment is only $898, rather than the $911 in the owner-occupied example with 10% down in the previous chapter.

The rent received is reported as taxable income from which you can deduct nearly all of your mortgage payments, including both the taxes and insurance. Because these deductions are reported on Schedule E (rental property), they are not subject to the limitations on personal tax deductions, and you can still take the standard deduction. The only portion that is not deductible is the principal reduction which is very small in the earlier years ($120/month or so).

You can also deduct "depreciation" which is a non-cash accounting deduction that will further reduce your taxable income. The improvements (buildings, not land) on residential property can be deducted over a period of 27½ years.

Assuming the land is value at 20% of the purchase price, the other 80% can be depreciated. So, 80% times $168,800 divided by 27½, gives us an annual non-cash depreciation deduction of $4,910 each year, even though the property may be appreciating in value.

To the extent your deductions exceed your rental income, you can deduct the difference from your other income (including your earned income), provided you are involved in the active management of the property.

In our example, we will assume that over the holding period (2000 to 2018) that the rent and tax savings was sufficient to pay the out of pocket expenses (mortgage payment, etc.) of the rental home.

As in our earlier example, in 2018 the property would be worth $337,000, for a gain of $168,200 ($337,000-168,800). Your loan balance in 2018 would be about $85,000, which means your equity (fair market value less mortgage balance) would be $252,000.

However, if the property were sold, the principal residence exemption would not be applicable, and the gain would be taxed at 15%, or $25,230.

In addition, the depreciation taken through the date of sale would be taxed at perhaps 25%. If the annual depreciation deduction was $4,910 per year and had been taken for 18 years, that $88,000 would be taxed at 25% for another $22,020 of tax, for a total tax on sale of $47,325.

Furthermore, if on sale in early 2018 there was a 6% real estate commission, the net proceeds on sale would be calculated as indicated on the following page:

Sales price	$337,000
Less loan balance	-85,000
Less commission	-20,000
Less taxes	- 47,325

Cash at closing	$184,475

So, in this example, our original upfront cost of $40,000 grew to $184,475 after tax, for a total annualized return of 9.74%. And this return was earned during a period in which the "Great Recession" took place! Because of the larger down payment and tax on the gain, the rental property return is not as great as the return of 14% on the owner-occupied home in the previous chapter.

How Millionaires Are Made: On the other hand, even a 9.74% annualized return is very substantial return. For example, $10,000 invested at 9.74% per annum for 30 years would grow to $162,535! These calculations may help explain why more millionaires are created through investments in real estate than any other means.

Cautions: To be fair in this analysis, I should note several things:

(1) Buying, renting, and maintaining a rental property does take time, money, and energy.

(2) To realize your gain, the property would have to be sold or refinanced, which would incur some costs.

(3) The actual rate of return does decline slowly as the equity in the property increases.

Single Family Homes: Single family home investments are available to almost anyone. It does not take a lot of initial capital nor does it take a lot of experience. As you read on, you will discover how and why so many people have found investing in single family homes so successful. There are many good reasons why this is so.

1. It's Easy. Single family homes are the easiest real estate investment to buy, to manage, and to sell. Only vacant land offers less management considerations. Rental homes are also subject to less governmental control and restrictions than multi-unit apartments.

2. Loans: You can usually obtain more favorable financing on single-family homes than on almost any other type of real estate other than owner-occupied homes. Many people end up with a rental home when they buy another (often larger) home to occupy as their primary residence, keeping the old home as a rental.

3. Appreciation and Yield: It is appreciation to a large degree, and not the rent, that helps you earn rates of return of 10% or greater on your invested dollar. Rents make your mortgage payment, and after the mortgage is paid off, may then provide significant cash flow for retirement or other purposes.

Notwithstanding the significant decline in average single family home prices in many parts of the country during the Great Recession, the long term trend must be up as inflation and government regulations make the cost of new homes increasingly expensive. Increases in population will also contribute to demand. As discussed earlier, the "principal residence" capital gains exclusion discussed earlier does not apply to rental properties. However, if you move into your rental property and occupy it as your principal residence for 24 months, then you can use the exclusion on sale, provided you hadn't used the exclusion on another property during the two years prior to sale.

4. Safety: There is an old stock market maxim which goes something like this: A conservative buyer should buy into a company that sells a product which will always be in demand. This same principle is what makes residential real estate, particularly rental homes, a very sound and safe investment. People will always require shelter.

5. Liquidity: Single family homes are more liquid (convertible into ready cash) than almost any other type of real estate. Priced realistically, a single family home can be sold quickly at a fair market price. Such liquidity may be lacking with other types of real estate investments. One big advantage of owning several single family homes over one multi-unit property is that liquidity is available on just part of your total investment.

For example, Investor A owns five rental homes with a combined equity of $500,000. Investor B owns a 10 unit apartment with equity of $500,000. If either investor needs $100,000 cash, which investor has the best options? Investor B would have only two real choices: He would have to sell his entire apartment complex or he would have to take out a costly second loan. Investor A could sell just one of his homes, and that sale would not affect his other four rental homes.

6. Tax Shield: What other investment can give you both a tax shield through the income tax deduction of depreciation (a non-cash deductible expense) and a huge profit on your investment? And with each single family home being a separate entity with its own tax base, you can manage the sale of your properties as in a chess match to give you the most desirable results.

For instance, you could sell one of the properties in a year in which you otherwise had very low income, resulting, perhaps, in less tax on sale.

Alternatively, holding several properties offers significant tax shelter of your other income. It doesn't take too many properties to significantly reduce your state and federal income tax liability legally.

7. Scarcity: The inexpensive single family home is not being built fast enough in most communities to meet consumer demands. In fact, in many parts of the country the inexpensive home is not even being built at all as builders continue to construct larger and more expensive homes that return a greater profit.

The blame often belongs not so much on the builders, but on local governments, which continue to add more and more building requirements which in turn lead to higher building expenses and thus ultimately higher prices for existing homes. Inflation in building materials and construction labor also adds to the cost of new homes.

The net result is that few new homes are being built that low-to-moderate income families can afford to buy. But the demand from both tenants and first-time home buyers for inexpensive property grows stronger over time, thus helping to push prices (and rents) upwards. Needless to say, this situation creates a profitable opportunity for investors.

8. Less Expensive to Buy: The required minimum down payment when purchasing a single family home costs the investor far less than the down payment to buy vacant land, commercial real estate or multi-family property.

Financing is typically available for 90% or more of the purchase price of an owner-occupied home, and 80% or more of a rental property.

Once you purchase a primary residence and you move in, you can always buy another "owner-occupied home" later and move into it. A year later you can repeat the repeat the process. I know of one investor who purchased his first four rental properties this way, each with very favorable owner-occupied financing.

9. Higher Occupancy Rates: All of the previously described advantages of single family homes can be summed up in one word...DEMAND. People must have a roof over their heads! And survey after survey has shown that buyers and tenants alike consider the most desirable shelter to be the single family home.

Because of this demand, the traditional vacancy rates for single-unit homes have been very low. Recent government surveys show that the vacancy rates for single family homes are almost always lower than for multi-family property.

Getting Started: Sounds great, so how does a person get started?

The beauty of a single family home investment portfolio is that you don't need a lot of money or a big income to get started. Very possibly your biggest problem in getting started will be mental, not financial. You have to believe that you can significantly increase your net worth before you spend your first dime.

Once you have the right frame of mind, you must then make a commitment to yourself - a commitment that you will put in the time and effort that is needed to get started on an investment program.

If it makes you feel any better, I can tell you without reservation that the first home you buy will be the hardest. After your first purchase, things can really start to snowball.

A Slow Starter: George took two years to purchase his first home, but when completed, he felt so inspired that he actually purchased six additional rental homes during the next twelve months. Today George owns 20 single family homes plus one 14 unit apartment building. His net worth is over five million dollars.

You can make money in real estate no matter what your job and income are. Sure, it helps to have $50,000 or so in the bank. And it would be nice if you were making $8,000 more per month. But you don't need to. You can really get started with little or no down payment and an income of $30,000 a year or less.

Recommended Books: Robert Allen authored an excellent book many years ago titled Nothing Down. This book teaches investors how to purchase real estate with little or nothing as a down payment. It's a book that any serious real estate investor should read. Three other books are also recommended:

1. The Monopoly Game by Dave Glubetich (out of print, but used copies available through Amazon.com)

2. How to Manage Real Property Successfully - in your Spare Time by Albert J. Lowry

3. How I turned $3,000 into a Million in Real Estate - in My Spare Time by William Nickerson.

It is interesting that many of these books refer to "in your spare time" as one of the keys to successful real estate investing.

Buy Your Own Home First: I strongly recommend buying your own home first. It is an excellent starting point. You can live in an apartment, however, and still make considerable money in rental homes.

For most people, though, owning their home is the first step. A modest home can be purchased with a minimum down payment. Within a few years you may have amassed enough equity so that you can borrow against the home and come up with enough money for a down payment on your first rental property.

Another strategy would be to buy another home as your new residence, and rent out your first home. You can usually obtain better terms and a lower interest rate when purchasing a house that will be owner-occupied than trying to finance a rental home.

As a homeowner you will also have established a good credit rating, assuming you make all of your payments on time. A good credit rating can mean better terms when financing your next purchase.

Moving On Up: I know of a few investors who are making a small fortune by buying a new primary residence every year or two with low down payment loans. They buy a home, move in, fix it up during the first year, and then rent it out and buy another property, starting the whole process all over again.

This can be a lot of work, but for the handyman type who enjoys remodeling, or is serious about learning, and doesn't mind living in a home while it is being remodeled, and doesn't mind moving every year or two, this method can be very profitable within just a few years.

Mortgages Paid Off: Many investors have found that after investing in single family homes for a decade or so, they can sell one home and use the proceeds to pay off several of their other mortgages. Many rental home investors end up with all their mortgages paid off in less than twenty years as a result of this strategy. This strategy could be important when planning your retirement.

No Current Tax On Gain: Lastly, you are not taxed on the gains each year as your properties appreciate in value. You are only taxed when a property is sold, and even then you are taxed at lower rates than other forms of income. For instance, the maximum long-term capital gains tax rate for couples filing jointly with income under $479,000 in 2018 is only 15%.

Have No Money? Let's say you don't have much money. Where can you get investment money? For the person who really wants to get started in investing in single family homes, here are several ways you can find your beginning capital:

1. Conventional Borrowing Methods: Almost anyone with decent credit and a steady job or income can borrow money. The only problem here is security. Most lending institutions want some type of security for their loan.

Without loan security, your bank may limit you to a maximum personal loan of, say, $5,000. With security (such as a free and Moreover, there is no tax on the first $38,600 of long term capital gain. row anywhere from 50 percent to 70 percent of the value.

If your bank is not the answer, try your life insurance policy. If your insurance is of the whole life equity-building variety, (rather than straight term) then you can obtain a lower interest rate loan from the insurance company than you would be able to from the bank. Don't overlook credit unions. Many make generous loans that are at a lower interest rate than banks. If you participate in a 401(k) plan at work, you may be able to borrow the down payment from your account at a reasonable rate, which, of course, is, in effect, paid to yourself!

Your best borrowing source might be an understanding relative. Depending on your relationship with your relatives, these might be the first people that you should ask.

To keep it on a business level, they can even be made silent partners in your investments.

2. Your Current Residence: If you own your home, and have more than 30 percent equity in it (for example, a value of $200,000 with a remaining mortgage loan of $140,000), then you can use your home to borrow the money for the down payment on your next property, either by refinancing your first mortgage or taking out a second mortgage or line of credit.

I recommend that investors refinance their home only when they have plenty of equity (more than 40 percent), have a bright employment future, and have a firm and sure investment goal in which all the money obtained from refinancing is accounted for.

Too many young adults these days refinance their mortgage, pay off their credit cards, and then spend the remainder on a new car or whatever. The money that could have gone to purchase a rental property is now sitting in their driveway (in the form of a car) or on a table in the living room (in the form of a widescreen TV). Instead of investing in an appreciating asset, they choose to "invest" in depreciating assets (assets which tend to lose significant value over time.

Borrowing via a second mortgage or deed of trust is sometimes a better answer than refinancing. The interest rates may be higher on the new loan, but by using a second mortgage you are able to keep the low interest rate first mortgage.

3. Lease Options: The lease option technique allows you buy at today's prices, but not pay until the end of the lease term. Here are the basics of this lease option technique:

Find a property that needs cosmetic work (painting, carpeting, etc.) but no major remodeling. Submit an offer to buy on a lease option with the purchase price to be paid in full twelve to twenty four months later.

It helps if you can buy the home for considerably less than market value price and have your financing at least semi-approved in advance.

4.   **Rapid Savings:** Many people have a hard time saving even $50 a month. I am not going to try to tell you it is easy, because it isn't. Let me tell you about my friend John. John wanted some advice on investing in real estate so he invited me out for dinner.

We started talking about down payments and John complained about not being able to save any money. He had three glasses of wine with dinner. I, of course, drank water - tap water - not water in those fancy bottles for $4.00. At $7 per glass, that wine cost John over $25 and with taxes and tip.

I mentioned to him the importance of watching every penny he spends. When I suggested that things like the wine might be draining his pocketbook, he seemed offended and said, "Yeah, but I only do it a couple of times a week. I work hard and deserve it!"

That was my first dinner at a sit-down restaurant in over a month. John obviously goes out a couple of times a week. He probably spends $400 more each month than I do on food and drink. That's almost $5,000 per year! With that attitude I suspect he is rather reckless in his other spending habits as well. After hearing his comment, I decided offering John advice on savings was a waste of time.

During the rest of the meal we spoke primarily about our children. Interestingly, I wrote this book to help people just like John to hopefully change their thinking and get control of their financial affairs.

But for those of you who do not yet own rental property, but want to, here are some suggestions. Keep in mind that once you buy a property and your equity begins to increase, your second purchase becomes much easier because you now have a source (through second mortgages or refinancing) to raise cash for the next purchase and you are familiar with the procedure to purchase property. It simply becomes easier and easier.

The Crash Cash Program: If you want to become rich or if you just want to enjoy the financial rewards earned by modest real estate investors, then consider a one-year crash program to raise enough money to buy your first home. But don't wait more than a year, because homes in your area may be appreciating in value at 5% per year or more (that's $10,000 on a $200,000 home).

Here are some ideas to help you get started on the one-year painful savings plan:

1. Start with the amount of money you and your spouse, if married, are normally able to save in a typical month. Let's say this amount is $200.

2. Next resolve to sacrifice for the next year. Give up most of your drinking or all of your smoking or most of your entertainment. Then cut your food budget by 1/3. Cut down on everything that is not a fixed expense. Let's assume that you can save an additional $400 a month this way. Just keep in mind that this is not a permanent way of life - only a one-year sacrifice.

3. Add up all of your installment loans such as car, credit cards, etc. If, for instance, your total account balances come to $10,000 and your total monthly payments are $550, then go see your local banker about what is called a debt consolidation loan. If your credit is good, you should be able to get a three year personal loan. That loan may require payments of about $350 a month, saving you another $200 per month.

4. Now that your entertainment budget has been slashed, you are going to have to find something else to do with your spare time. Why not take up a hobby that can make you extra money, or do babysitting, or piano teaching, yard mowing, or consulting? If you stop and think about it, you can probably come up with many ways to earn an extra $400 a month. Here's what our mythical couple have saved:

Normal Savings	$ 200
Sacrificial savings	$ 400
Consolidated loans	$ 200
Extra earned income	$ 400

Total savings of	$1,200

$1,200 times 12 months equals $14,400. With interest, these funds might grow to about $15,000 by the end of the first year. Now if $15,000 can get you started with your first (or even a second) home in your community - then great.

Your one year of sacrifices will be over and you will be able to reap some of the great benefits found with single family home investments. But if you are still a little short financially, consider continuing your crash savings program for another year.

The Real Secret To Savings: The real secret to getting this plan to work is to **not buy anything unless absolutely necessary**. It is the same secret we discussed earlier about getting out of debt.

Keep a written record each day of not only your expenditures, but also of the things you were tempted to buy, but didn't. Do this for at least one or two months. At the end of each month, review your written records carefully. Hopefully, this will provide a record of your achievements and provide the motivation to continue your savings plan.

Leverage: Leverage and appreciation are the key elements in real estate investing. Leverage simply means controlling the most property with the least amount of money. The greater your skill in using leverage, the greater will be the return on your dollar invested over time. We have already discussed somewhat how this principle can create wealth for you almost overnight.

Let's say I buy a vacant lot for $100,000, and let's ignore property taxes and any income. Let's assume the property increases (appreciates) 10% in value during the first year. Had I paid all cash for the property, my annual rate of return would have been 10%. My investment would have been $100,000, and my profit would have been $10,000. $10,000/$100,000 = 10%. The math is really quite simple.

Instead, let's say you buy the same vacant lot for $100,000 by obtaining a 90% mortgage at 7%. At the end of the first year, your appreciation is still $10,000, but you have to pay interest of $6,300 (7% of $90,000). Therefore, your profit is only $3,300. But because you invested only $10,000 of your own money, the profit of $3,300 on a $10,000 investment equals an annual rate of return of 33%!

Of course, leverage can work against you. If the property increased in value only 5%, or $5,000 and your interest payment was $6,300, you would have lost $1,700 of your equity, for a negative 17% return on your $10,000 investment. The all-cash buyer would still have a positive 10% rate of return.

Another interesting aspect about real estate investing is that even if the value has dropped significantly, as values did during the Great recession, you are not forced to sell as long as you make your mortgage payments.

You can use leverage when buying stocks (called a margin account), but if the stock values drop significantly, the brokerage firm will liquidate your investments to pay off the loan. That does not happen in real estate, so even if the market value of your home drops temporarily, you can still keep your home, and then enjoy the potential increase in value in the years to come.

For instance, those who purchased homes in the early 2000's saw their values drop during the Great Recession, often well below their purchase price. If they continued making their mortgage payments and still own the property today, they are generally quite pleased with their purchase.

Judicial use of leverage should allow you to multiply your gains in good years sufficiently to more than offset the losses in bad years. Leverage is one of the essential success factors, especially if you want to make above average returns when investing in rental homes.

Inflation: Inflation is a term used to refer to the general increase in the level of prices over time. Some inflation can be good for the economy, and the government uses monetary policy to try to control the rate of inflation.

The cost of almost everything has increased during the past several decades, although not always at a constant rate. Talk to your parents or any "old-timer" and they will tell you about what milk, gasoline, or whatever used to cost decades ago. Inflation reduces the purchasing power of the dollar as things cost more.

Rising prices caused by inflation can certainly be a serious problem for the consumer. But to the real estate investor, inflation can be an ally and well-located homes have increased at a rate above the inflation rate; homes in less desirable locations at less than the inflation rate.

Although we had some "deflation," or at least stagnation, in the value of housing during the Great Recession of 2008 to 2012, the average sales price of housing throughout the U.S. is on the rise again. If history teaches us anything, it seems that an average 3% to 5% annual increase in home values during the next 12 years is a realistic projection. Every time a carpenter or a bricklayer receives a new contract for higher wages, the price of new homes goes up a notch. Every time lumber prices or energy costs increase, the price of new homes goes up a notch. And just like the shadow that follows your body, the prices of used homes follow right along with the price of new homes.

Got To Live Somewhere: A pessimist may tell you that the fact that your house has increased greatly in value doesn't make any difference because even if you sell it, you still have to live somewhere. But what if you had 5 rental houses?

A few years ago I visited an upscale condominium complex. I asked the listing broker about who were the potential buyers. He told me his entire market is people near retirement age who want to sell their large houses and move to a smaller, maintenance free environment.

206

The broker told me that they even offered a program to help people sell their houses. I asked if he ever had apartment dwellers purchase a condo, to which he replied, "Of course not. Anyone who has lived in an apartment during the past ten years simply hasn't saved enough to purchase even our least expensive condo, which sells for $320,000."

Paying Off Your mortgage: Most people realize how important it is to have your home mortgage paid off before you retire. That may even be the number one priority for a comfortable retirement.

Many financial planners will advise you to remain in other investments rather than prepay your mortgage. With the low interest rates in 2013, and the S&P 500 index increasing at over 20% during 2013, that may have make sense. But a major drop in the market, as we saw in 2008, however, could be disruptive to your retirement plans.

Another argument against prepaying your mortgage is that the interest is tax deductible. That may have been true in the past, but with the increased standard deduction of $24,000 (married) in 2018, that may no longer be true.

Moreover, many taxpayers approaching retirement find that the interest deduction, when combined with other deductions, is just enough to make it worthwhile to itemize their deductions. In other words, they are receiving very little benefit from the deduction, and as additional principal is paid, it may be to their benefit to take the standard deduction, in which case there is no advantage to the deductibility of the interest paid.

Prepaying a mortgage gives you a "guaranteed" rate of return as the mortgage will eventually be paid off anyway. If your interest rate is, say 5%, then that is a "guaranteed" 5% return on your investment.

If you do not itemized your deductions on your income tax return, that interest savings equates to a 5% AFTER TAX return!

Paid Off Sooner: The amount you prepay on your mortgage means that your mortgage will be paid off sooner, even though your monthly payment does not change. Here are a few examples. Let's assume that you purchased your home five years ago with an original mortgage of $200,000 with fixed interest rate of 5%:

Lump Sum: If you made a lump sum payment of $15,000, your mortgage would be paid off 42 months sooner, saving you $30,521 in interest!

Increased monthly payment: If you increased your monthly payment by an additional $100 each month, the mortgage would be paid off 43 months sooner, saving you $21,951 in interest payments.

Many investors have developed an amortization table in Microsoft Excel that allows them to make these and other calculations. Even if you decide to invest in other investments for the time being, you can use the amortization schedule to calculate how much you will need in those other investments to pay off your mortgage when you plan to retire.

Keeping Ahead of Inflation: When your money is invested in real estate, you will have more than a hedge against inflation. You will have an investment that in most years will keep you AHEAD of inflation. If you bury your money in a tin can in the back yard, obviously inflation will rob you of purchasing power. But many other investments do not bring a high enough return to even keep up with the cost of living index in most years, most notably savings accounts and certificates of deposit.

I am not attempting to justify inflation, but rather to show you how it can be used to help you make money. A steady rate of inflation between 3 and 5 per cent is a healthy factor from a real estate standpoint. As discussed earlier, leverage can magnify those rates based upon your initial investment.

But when homes appreciate at over 10% per year, as happened in some of the hotter markets in the 2003 to 2006 period, it is not a good thing because a short cooling-off period is bound to follow, and in fact that is what happened during the Great Recession (2008 to 2011). Steady growth is the best.

Even though I told you that with modest inflation rates you can reap big profits, you should not base an investment program solely on rising prices. Rental homes can be profitable investments at even zero appreciation. Buying and selling correctly, combined with good leverage, and maximizing your rental income and minimizing your expenses through a sound management, will still make you money. Inflation only sweetens the pot a little as you can buy more homes on a faster time schedule.

Other Factors: Residential real estate appreciation rates tend to be somewhat in excess of the Cost-of-Living Index increases, especially in cities, even smaller ones, which are growing in population. There are many reasons why this is so. Here are three more reasons why home prices in most communities will increase in value over the next ten years:

1. Increasing Population: You have heard all the talk about smaller families, etc. But don't be fooled. Our population is still growing. People are living longer; our birth rate still exceeds our death rate; our population is growing rapidly through both legal and illegal immigration.

The net result is an addition of more than 5,000 people every day, and that should result in even more pressure on the price of housing.

2.   New Property Economics: New housing starts are far short of meeting that demand. New housing starts spurt and sputter. When interest rates are low new building starts will begin to reach the needed levels. But low prices for existing houses tends to limit the ability of builders to sell new homes, or at least until the prices of older homes have caught up with the prices of new homes.

3.   Governmental Restrictions: Stricter building codes, more expensive union contracts, and more red tape in building a new home will also result in higher prices, which eventually increases the prices paid for existing housing.

What does all this mean? There will be more homebuyers and more tenants. There is a lesson to be learned here: Do not be afraid to buy real estate.

Rentals Close To Home: Of course the rental property does not have to be next door, but I prefer rental properties close to where I live. If you buy multiple rentals, you should prefer that they all to be within a mile or two of each other. Rental property does take time to show to potential renters, to maintain, and to repair. If the rental property is close to your home, all this becomes much easier. If you hire someone to manage them, even cut the yards, it is easier and cheaper if the rental properties are fairly close together.

Frustration: Your success in owning rental property is partly how you live with what I call the frustration factor. My father could have never been a successful real estate investor. He would lose sleep over a broken dishwasher.

Yes, you have to watch your pennies, otherwise the dollars slip away. But you have to consider the big picture. Replacing a $500 dishwasher is a relatively minor expenditure in the big picture.

For instance, if your $250,000 rental house appreciated only 4% in a year, that $10,000 added to your net worth! Is the $500 dishwasher worth losing sleep over? My father would have tried to charge the tenant for the dishwasher, even though the dishwasher was over 12 years old. My father would have still had to pay for the dishwasher. The tenant would be unhappy and maybe even moved out.

Attention To Detail: In the rental property business, close attention to detail is important. The classic example of this actually happened to my brother. His bedroom door apparently was loose. I mentioned that he should tighten the hinges, but he did not have a screwdriver handy. Three weeks later the door worked its way loose and knocked a hole in the dry wall. For want of a $3 screwdriver, my brother ended up paying a handyman $300 to repair the drywall and re-hang the door!

Tenants As Customers: Tenants are like customers. You need to treat them fairly. You have entrusted property worth perhaps $250,000 to their care. Do you really want them mad at you?

Repairs: Another factor to consider is your ability to do the handyman work. Are you able to fix minor plumbing problems, replace an electrical switch? It helps if you are able to do some of these or can hire someone who can do them for you at a reasonable cost. Can you handle a significant remodel? Learning how to do these things can increase your return.

I was never very good at these things, so I purchased properties that were in above-average physical condition in above-average neighbor-hoods.

I felt this would minimize my repair costs and minimize my rental headaches. In addition, such homes are likely to attract better tenants.

This has proven to be a good strategy for me, as I also had a full time job. I have had several tenants who have rented from me for fifteen years or more!

On the other hand, if you are good at minor repairs and fixing up a home and have the time, consider the approach taken by William Nickerson as described in his book, How I turned $1,000 into a Million in Real Estate - in my Spare Time. Published in 1959, the book has remained a classic, and although the dollars mentioned need to be mentally adjusted to reflect subsequent inflation, the concepts described in that book are still valid today.

That book has probably created more millionaires than any other book in investing history. It simply is a masterpiece of common sense advice, no matter what type of investing you are contemplating. What makes Nickerson's book so good?

His writings are crammed full with practical and real guidance on real estate investing with a proven technique for making money that really works. No get-rich-quick hype. No motivation speeches or excessive cheerleading. No nothing-down promises of instant wealth or easy profits. Just tons of genuine advice real estate investors need to hear. Nickerson prepared readers for what actually exists in the modern real estate world."

Sadly, William Nickerson died in 2000. He wrote books on other subjects but he will always be known for his original 1959 real estate masterpiece and its later revisions that also contain much more information than his original book.

Fixer-Uppers: Mr. Nickerson's method of making money in real estate was essentially to buy run down houses and small apartments in good neighborhoods, fix them up, then rent them for considerably more than they were rented for prior to the renovation. Such properties are often valued at a multiple of rental income. If you were able to increase rents by 20% - or reduce expenses by 20%, the building would be worth perhaps 20% more.

Thus, after fixing them up, William had several options: First, rent them out at the higher rent and retain the cash flow after making the mortgage payments. Second, refinance the property with a larger loan. This would require that all of the increased cash flow be used to repay the mortgage, but would give him considerable operating capital to buy more properties and fix them up.

A third option would be to sell the property for the higher value and invest the difference between the increased value and the original mortgage in additional properties. A tax-deferred exchange makes this selling option even more attractive because it allows you to move into more expensive or multiple-unit properties without have to pay any capital gains tax on the sale.

Cash Flow: So, that was Mr. Nickerson's approach, and in the 1950's the name of the game was increasing cash flow by fixing up the property. During the past 30 years, the name of the game has been inflation, also called appreciation. Over several decades, the average home in most metropolitan areas has increased in value (on average) by a rate slightly greater than inflation.

Holding Period: Generally, the shorter the holding period, the greater the return, ignoring transaction costs. That may not be realistic, you say. Shouldn't selling costs and capital gains taxes be considered to give an after tax return?

Of course they should be considered. That is why we suggest that the appreciation during a short holding period may be insufficient to recover the selling commission of perhaps 6% and other closing costs.

Tax Free Exchanges: Section 1031 of the Internal Revenue Code allows the owner of an investment property to do a tax free (actually it is tax deferred) exchange. No, that does not mean that you have to find someone who has a property you want and who also wants your property. You can sell your property just as you would normally do, except you have the cash proceeds escrowed with a title company or other independent intermediary.

You then have 45 days to identify the property you wish to buy, and six months (from your sale date) to actually close on the purchase. If you meet these and possibly other requirements, you do not have to pay tax on the gain. In effect, your basis ("cost" for calculating depreciation and for calculating the gain when the new property is sold) in the new property is reduced by the amount of the deferred gain.

The two properties must be "like kind" properties and a personal residence does not qualify. Nevertheless, an apartment can be exchanged for vacant land, as long as both are held for investment purposes. You can even exchange a rental property for a home you plan to reside in later on if you use it as a rental property for a year or more before moving into it. You can also do an exchange to defer just part of the gain.

In our next chapter we will offer some advice for the first time buyer of a single family home. Even an experienced investor may find this chapter profitable.

***

Advice for the First Time Buyer

"It's tough to become financially free with passive investing.
Real estate investing is active investing. It's not for the lazy.
Too many people would rather write a check to strangers to manage -
and hope for the best - than to take control themselves."

Here is some additional advice on buying your first property, regardless of whether it is to be your home or a rental property:

Location: When looking for your first home, select the neighborhood you would prefer to live in. This is good advice even if the property is to be a rental. Buying a house 'across the tracks' because its price is lower is generally a poor strategy. A house in a weaker neighborhood is likely to attract weaker tenants; that means higher turnover, more vacancy, more damage, and more maintenance. By buying a rental in a nicer neighborhood, you tend to attract better tenants, have fewer repairs, and, ultimately, you will probably have greater appreciation.

Close to Home: If you already own your own home, buy rental properties close by. It is much easier to show the property to a prospective tenant, fix a plumbing problem, or paint the front porch, if the house is next door, rather than across town.

A tenant is more likely to take care of a house if he knows you live a few blocks away. You probably selected your home because of the neighborhood; if you find the neighborhood desirable, so will prospective tenants and, perhaps more importantly, future purchasers.

Use A Real Estate Broker: A good real estate agent who is familiar with your target neighborhood can be very helpful, especially when you are buying your first property. The agent can point out the positives and negatives about a property. Not that you can't do this on your own, but four eyes are usually better than two.

The agent may be able to give some ideas on fixing up the property, can recommend a structural engineer to evaluate foundation problems, or a termite inspector, or other professionals to help you evaluate the property either before or in connection with making an offer.

An agent can help explain the "standard commission approved" contract to you, so that you will understand the terms used and typical provisions and conditions, as well as the timing of what the seller and you as the buyer must do. The agent can explain how contingencies work.

Earnest Money: Most sellers require a deposit of earnest money with the acceptance of the contract. This is a small deposit of perhaps $2,000 to $5,000 to be held by the brokerage firm or title insurance company until closing. It is usually non-refundable if you default on the contract. If certain contingencies are not met, the funds may be refundable.

Contingencies: Two typical contingencies might be the buyer's approval of a home inspection report and the buyer obtaining acceptable financing. Both of these allow you to get your earnest money back if the inspection is negative or you are unable to obtain the loan described in the contingency clause.

Conflicting Objectives: While working with a real estate agent can be beneficial, keep in mind your objectives may conflict with his objectives. His objective is to earn a commission by getting you to purchase a house. If you don't buy a house through him, he does not earn a commission.

The agent's commission is substantial, perhaps half of a 6% commission, or $6,000 on a $200,000 house, and is almost always paid by the seller. The more you pay for a house, the greater his commission. The less time he spends with you, the greater his "hourly" earnings. Your objective is to view a lot of houses, make low offers, and get the best deal you can make.

Look at Many Properties: It's important when buying your first home (or any rental property, for that matter), not to fall in love with the first or second home you see. A good agent can help set up appointments to view the houses in your selected neighborhood that meet your specific criteria. With proper planning, you can inspect several homes in a just a few hours.

For instance, if you are looking for your first home and have two children, with a third one on the way, you will probably want a four-bedroom home. Perhaps you may need a two-car garage.

In many cities you can access the multi-list service on the Internet and perform your own search. You can look at the descriptions, and perhaps even drive by the properties. Then ask your agent to set up an appointment to view a few of those properties.

In many communities the listing agents (the agents working with the seller) attempt to sell their listing with open houses. That is a great way to become more familiar with your neighborhood, the types of houses on the market, the prices at which they are being offered, etc.

In many neighborhoods you can visit five to ten properties in one afternoon. Even if you find a house on your own you want to buy, it may be advisable to work through your agent, again for the reasons mentioned above.

The internet (or your agent) can also help you follow up on what the property ultimately sold for. Literally, within a month, you can become an expert in your selected neighborhood.

I usually advise people to do what I did when I started out, and that is to view at least ten properties before making your first offer. Make your first offer for considerably less than the asking price. If the seller finds it unacceptable, he can always make a counter-offer to your offer. Moreover, you can always increase your offer later.

The Typical Home: When screening properties you would consider buying, it may be helpful to set additional criteria. For instance, in the neighborhood in which I bought many of my properties, most of the homes were on 50 foot wide lots, so I ruled out smaller lots. Most homes were brick, so I ruled out frame houses. Most houses had a one or two car garage, so I ruled out houses without a garage. I ruled out houses on busy streets, houses that looked weird or didn't fit in with the neighborhood. I also ruled out oversized and undersized houses. In other words, I looked only at the typical home in the neighborhood.

When viewing a number of properties, it may be advisable to take along a digital camera so you can take pictures of the features you like and don't like, or just wish to remember, of each house. Your first picture at each house should be of the front showing the address.

I have seen some people actually use the macro feature on their camera or phone and shoot a picture of the listing sheet. Take perhaps 10 or more pictures of each house, some exterior, and some interior. That will allow you to remember each property better.

Collect data: The more systematic your collection of data about your selected neighborhood is, the more likely you are to find undervalued properties. If your goal is to buy a good home at a price well under market value, you need to look at lots of homes and, more importantly, make lots of offers.

Multiple Offers: I used to make 3 or 4 offers after inspecting perhaps ten homes over a weekend. I couldn't close on four homes at once if all four offers were accepted, so I relied on a contingency clause which gave me a short period of time to get out for any or no reason, such as making the offer subject to approval by my wife within two days of the seller's acceptance of my offer.

More often than not, I would have all four offers rejected, sometimes without even a counter-offer. But because I knew my market well, and because I made low offers, I knew that if any offer was accepted, I was probably getting a good deal.

In retrospect, the price paid for a property may not make that much difference. Several years ago I sold a house for $480,000 that I had bought 25 years ago for $52,000. So whether I had paid $52,000, $50,000, or $55,000 for it didn't make that much difference. I am just thankful that I bought that house, and I ask myself why I didn't buy more houses!

Recent Listings: A couple of hints about making low-ball offers: First, it is usually a waste of time if the house has been on the market for only a few weeks. The listing agent recently convinced the seller that his property is worth close to the asking price, and maybe even more, so as to get the listing. The broker may now be reluctant to submitting a low offer, and the buyer may be equally reluctant to accept one.

After the property has been on the market for a couple of months with no offers, the seller may be more motivated to accept a low offer. Your real estate agent can usually find out how long a property has been on the market and its listing price history.

Second Hint: If the house is empty, the seller may be more motivated to accept a low offer. If the seller has purchased a new house, perhaps even moved out-of-state, and is now facing two mortgage payments, he may be far more likely to accept a low offer than the seller who still lives in the home and plans to buy a new home only after his home sells.

Third Hint: In most of the U.S., December and January are typically good months to make low offers, as real estate sales are slow in these months, utility bills are high, etc. I suspect in Phoenix and Miami, just the opposite is true, with June and July being slow sales months.

Fourth Hint: Your agent can also discover information about the seller through the listing agent to help you in making an acceptable offer. I bought a house once where the sellers were still living in their home, but were having a home custom built to accommodate their growing family. The new home would not be completed for four months.

I made a low offer that they accepted because I agreed to let them lease it back from me for as long as they needed (with some reasonable restrictions, of course) until their new house was completed and they were ready to move. Since I was going to use the property as a rental property anyway, their stay was not inconsistent with my objectives, as long as I got a good price.

Fifth Hint (and perhaps the best): When you submit your offer include an explanation as to why you feel your price is a fair price (even if you know it is low!) List all the negatives about the property, such as unusable space, poor landscaping, needs painting, new carpet, new roof, kitchen needs remodeling, a house down the street just sold for considerably less - Get the picture?

I wrote a letter just like I described; the property was offered at $260,000, which was probably a fair price. I offered $210,000, and included a letter describing all of the negative aspects of the property. The owner came over to my house and went into a tirade about why my letter was wrong. I didn't argue much, just listened. And after she called me several derogatory names, she asked me if I would be willing to pay $220,000. I agreed, and we later actually became friends.

What I didn't realize at the time, but discovered later, was that she and her husband had bought and renovated three houses, and all three were on the market and not selling, and their lender was making cash demands on their short term loans. They had discovered the old maxim: A bank is a place where they lend you an umbrella in fair weather and then ask it back when it starts to rain.

My offer and fast closing got them out of a tight financial situation, and, more importantly, I was able to buy the house for perhaps 10% under its fair market value. I am certain that I would not have purchased that property at such a bargain price if I hadn't made an offer. As hockey player, Wayne Gretzke, puts it, 'You always miss 100% of the shots you don't take.'

There is also a good possibility that I would not have purchased it for the low price if I hadn't pointed out many of the house's flaws. I might add that the flaws I mentioned were typical of the neighborhood and really didn't affect the value that much.

Consider also the price you can afford in terms of the down payment and mortgage payments. If the property is be a rental, consider how much rent you might be able to charge.

Of course, the more you pay for a house, the larger your down payment and the larger your mortgage payment, so getting a good price is important. But perhaps it is more important to at least buy something, and not just dream about it.

Mortgage Payments: For the reader's convenience I have included a Mortgage Payment Table in Appendix C of this book. It will help you calculate what the principal and interest payment will be on any loan. Because most lenders will want to escrow a monthly amount to cover the annual payments of property taxes and insurance, be sure to consider what those amounts might be in estimating your monthly payment.

Ask Questions: Also, don't be afraid to ask questions: A fool wonders; a wise man asks. One constant challenge of life is protecting ourselves from thinking that we know enough. Asking a question is a way of learning more, preparing better, and making better decisions. Every person you meet knows something that you don't; learn from them.

Try to associate with others who are buying rental properties. Discuss what they did right and what they did wrong. If you follow the advice offered above, you probably won't make any major mistakes, and might just find that diamond in the rough!

***

Conclusions, Updates, And Reflections

Wealth Accumulation: The road to asset accumulation, which I call wealth accumulation, begins with generating income, not spending all of that income, and then investing for acceptable returns.

The Magic Formula: The formula, in non-mathematical terms, is: Income + Frugal Spending = Savings; Savings times Investment = Wealth. Any person of modest means can accumulate significant wealth through the use of this formula. It's as simple as that.

Maximizing Income: To maximize your income, obtain an appropriate education or training. Then convince your employer to increase your salary by demonstrating loyalty and good work ethics. In your twenties, go for the money; in later years, follow your passions. Passions without education and work experience seldom prove to be profitable.

Passion: A desire is what you want to be without further action and commitment, as in "I want to be a doctor." A passion is desire plus action; as in "I am working as hard as I can to become a doctor." If that's your passion, then start by getting an A+ in high school biology. Study the text book to the extent that you know it better than your instructor. Volunteer at the local hospital. That's commitment. Unless you are prepared to commit yourself to the time and energy it takes to achieve those goals, the mere desire won't create any income nor lead to a rewarding career.

Controlling Expenditures: The secret to getting – or staying – out of debt is to control your expenditures. Don't buy something unless you really need it. A portion of everything you earn should be yours to keep and invest. Develop frugal habits. Six dollars a day not spent, but saved and invested at 5% will grow to over $100,000 in 25 years.

That's less than the cost of a pack of cigarettes or a glass of wine per day. Which would you rather have at 55 years of age: $100,000 or lung cancer? Even with no earnings, wouldn't you rather have the $54,750? Think about that the next time you buy a pack of cigarettes, or order a glass of wine, or spend even a small amount of money on something you don't really need.

Budgeting: Budgeting sounds great on paper, but it seldom works in practice. Writing down each expenditure each day for several months will help you see where your money is going and how to best control it. Moreover, knowing that you have to write it down, may make you think twice about whether to even spend the money!

Minimize Debt: Being in debt is a form of voluntary slavery in which much of your income – which should be yours to keep – goes to make loan and credit card payments. Student debt is particularly burdensome as it is one of the few debts that cannot be discharged in bankruptcy, and it can stay with you for a lifetime. There are now thousands of retired persons that are having a portion of their Social Security payments withheld to repay student loans from decades ago.

Good Debt: Going into debt to purchase assets which are likely to appreciate, such as a family home or education that is likely to lead to profitable employment, can be the first step toward wealth accumulation.

Bad Debt: Credit cards are almost necessary to have as a convenience, such as to buy gas or order anything online. The disadvantage is that they make it too easy to buy things you really don't need. If the card balance is not paid off in full each month, the interest can compound leading to an ever increasing portion of your income committed to paying off debt for items you probably didn't need anyway.

Borrowing for your education (taking out student loans) can be worthwhile if such studies prepare you for a decent paying job. Conversely, if you take out student loans to live on because you don't want to look for work, or if you don't major in a field of study that will lead to significantly greater income, then you have taken on bad debt that will be hard to pay back.

The Road to Ruin: Overspending is a double-edged sword, with both edges cutting against you. Not only does overspending reduce that which you have available to save and invest, but it also causes you to develop a life style that, in the long run, is beyond your means.

The frugal person is much better prepared to weather the several financial setbacks that most of us endure over our lifetimes. The frugal person not only has a larger cushion (savings) but also needs less to support his or her life style.

Want to Lose Your Job? Talk to any human resources person and they will tell you that two of the primary causes behind a person being fired for "poor performance" are personal money problems and divorce. Of course, money problems are also one of the primary contributors to divorce as well. This not only emphasizes the importance of frugality on job stability, but also the importance of marrying someone with similar financial goals.

Keep Your Payments Current: Missing a loan or credit card payment can cost you dearly, not only in late charges and interest, but also by hurting your credit score. For example: Let's say you purchase a home by obtaining a $200,000 loan. If the lender charges interest of 5.5% rather than 5% because of your missed credit card payments, you will pay an additional $62 per month or $744 per year, or over $22,000 over a thirty year period.

The Math: The chapter on "The Mathematics of Wealth Accumulation" is not likely to be part of your day-to-day activities, but was included to demonstrate the principles of both wealth accumulation and debt accumulation. The concept of compound interest was explored and, hopefully, will provide sufficient motivation to save and invest.

Frugality: Frugality is being wise about how you spend money on yourself. It has nothing to do with being cheap or dishonest. Frugality not only leads to wealth, but also to more options later on.

Value: The value of a possession is relative. All too often we place a high value on an impromptu purchase and less value on saving for the future. The joy of buying a $40,000 automobile fades rapidly, but the security of having that same $40,000 invested increases each year

Time Management: In our chapters on time management we learned how to get more done each day by creating to-do lists and then working on the more important ones first. The file card system has proven to be the most effective time management tool for most people. The good news is that the "Oh, I can remember" system works 50% of the time; the bad news is that it doesn't work 50% of the time! If it's important enough to work on, it is important enough to be written down on paper.

Goals: Setting long term goals, be they career development, home purchase, advanced education, or comfortable retirement, is the first step in reaching such goals. By writing those goals down and reviewing them periodically, you will be more effective in using your resources – your time, energy, and money – to accomplish those goals.

Having definite, specific goals can provide a great incentive to save and invest, but even if you have few specific goals currently, realize that you will likely have some in the future. If nothing else, consider setting a goal of saving enough to live on for one year in the event you were fired or quit your job – and without reducing your standard of living. Again, frugality helps in that it allows you to save more, and yet need less to continue your standard of living.

Taxes: Our chapter on taxation emphasized the differences in how income is taxed. Earned income, such as your salary, is generally taxed immediately and at significantly higher rates than long term capital gains on investments, which are taxed at lower rates and then only when the investment is sold. Our education yields currently taxable earned income; our investments can yield capital gains, the tax on which is deferred until sold, or perhaps not taxed at all.

Generally, there is no tax on up to $500,000 (married) of profit in the sale of your primary residence. If any investment is held until the owner's death, the gains pass income tax free to your family due to the tax concept commonly referred to as "step up in basis."

Actual tax rates, deductions, and rules change somewhat from time to time with the whims of Congress, but the structural differences in how earned income and capital gains are taxed have been embedded in our tax system for well over sixty years and are likely to continue well into the future.

Many commentators think the system is unfair, but as John F. Kennedy once said, "Life is unfair." Successful people understand that the taxation system may be unfair but they learn how it affects them. They then conduct their financial affairs so that the unfairness in taxation works to their advantage. They invest for capital gains!

Investments: Funds accumulated in a savings or check account may earn little interest (fully taxable), but may be necessary for immediate emergencies. The last several chapters of this book discussed how your unspent income (savings) could be invested for long term growth (capital gains) in either (or both) securities or real estate.

The S&P 500: We discussed how consistently investing in a low cost S&P 500 mutual fund or ETF (exchange traded fund), although not exciting, is likely over time to perform better than most any other type of stock or bond investment. Such investment offers broad diversification, tax efficiency, and the least amount of time commitment.

Nobody knows what the market will do tomorrow, next month, or even over the next year. However, as the economy continues to expand, even though at irregular rates, the stock market over time has significantly outperformed fixed rate investments, such as bonds and certificates of deposit.

Distraction: Don't be distracted by the day to day news about the stock market. Don't let that discourage you from investing. The changes in stock market values make the news every day. Those changes are quantitative and can be made to sound important. Plus there are always numerous "talking heads" – so-called experts – who can offer commentary to fill up the 24 hours of news being offered on numerous channels.

Listening to those experts on television, even for years, will not make you a better investor. All publicly-known knowledge about a company is usually already reflected in its stock price. To be a better investor, consider rereading Chapter 19 – "The Foolproof Method of Investing."

Real Estate: There are virtually no daily quotes on how "real estate" is doing and thus changes in real estate values seldom make the daily news. Even national statistics often have little to do with local markets. Moreover, there are no national sponsors of real estate investing as there are of securities investing. Charles Schwab, Merrill Lynch, Fidelity, and Vanguard can afford to advertise on national television. Your local real estate broker cannot.

It may come as a surprise to many business news listeners that the value of all real estate in the country far exceeds the value of all publicly-traded securities. In fact, the value of just residential housing is almost double the capitalized value of all companies listed on the New York Stock Exchange!

Additional real estate values would include commercial, office, business, government, and industrial properties, as well as farms and vacant land.

Your Home: For most people, your home should be your first real estate investment. Your savings goal should include not only the down payment but also an emergency fund to cover the many unexpected expenses that accompany home ownership.

Some will say that a home is not an investment. But ask any homeowner over fifty-five years of age, and most will tell you that the value of their home is a very significant part of, if not most of, their net worth.

Typical is the homeowner who purchased his home for $100,000 thirty years ago and today it is worth $250,000. If that homeowner sold it today, the entire $150,000 of gain would be income tax free. And all this came from what may have been a $10,000 down payment.

Rhetorical question: How many similarly situated persons who didn't purchase a home would have saved up $250,000 by not buying a home?

Rental Homes: The economics on rental homes are not as favorable as they are on an owner-occupied home due to the larger down payment required, slightly higher mortgage interest rate, and subsequent taxation of gain on sale of the rental home. Nevertheless, a rental home is usually the most profitable way – sometimes the only way – the average person can expand their real estate investments beyond their own home.

Your rental home(s) should be close to your own home to facilitate the management and the like. A tenant who lives across the street is more likely to pay his or her rent on time and take better care of the property than a tenant who lives on the other side of town. Just as location is important in selecting your own home, so it is with a rental home.

In most markets today, the rental income could just about cover the mortgage payment, including taxes and insurance. As rents increase, the income may more than cover all of the ownership expenses. As the value increases and the loan is paid down, your equity grows more and more each year. In almost any society around the globe, the person who owns his or her own home and a similar rental home free and clear of any mortgage can have a reasonable comfortable retirement.

But even with a relatively short holding period, the ownership of a rental home can prove to be quite profitable. One of the reasons is that the down payment is only a small percentage of the purchase price while the appreciation is on the entire value of the property.

For example, assume you put 20% down and the income covers the expenses and the value increases only 4% per year. During the first year that increase (before selling expenses) represents a 20% return on your equity. Other planning strategies may also be available to avoid or at least delay the taxation on any gain.

Softening of the Market: As I am finalizing this second edition of the book in 2018, real estate market appears to be softening in many locations. Many experts are predicting either a leveling off or slight decline during the next year or two. There are several reasons for this. In many cities home prices have risen more rapidly than consumer income, making houses less affordable. Interest rates have risen and are expected to rise gradually over the next few years. A few years ago the average interest rate on a new home loan was 3.5%; today it is 4.5%. That may not sound like much, but it amounts to an extra $115 per month on a $200,000 mortgage.

Furthermore, under the recent income tax changes most homeowners may not get any benefit from the deductibility of interest and property taxes. The increased standard deduction of $12,000 (single) and $24,000 (married) means that your deductions have to exceed that threshold before you receive any advantage for itemizing.

Moreover, there is a new $10,000 limitation on deductions for state and local taxes, such as income taxes and property taxes. This limitation will impact the owner-occupant, but won't affect the deductibility with respect to rental homes.

Nevertheless, higher interest rates and these tax changes could reduce the demand for single family homes and could affect long term appreciation rates.

On the other hand, any decline in housing prices over the next few years may present a perfect buying opportunity. Those who purchased homes in 2010 when prices were declining, are generally pleased with their purchases today, even though prices continued to decline in many markets for another year of two. In other words, don't let the stabilizing of the market deter you from buying your home or a rental home.

As our population grows and the government continues to print more money by increasing the national debt, there should be no doubt that the continued long term growth in housing prices is almost a certainty.

Location: Although the earlier chapters mentioned the importance of location, perhaps a further discussion is warranted. Location can mean everything from the city you live in, to the neighborhood, and even to the block you live on. Of course, the odds of appreciation would be in your favor if you invested in a growing city such as Denver, Las Vegas, or Austin. Even though the odds are against you in a city like Baltimore, whose population has been shrinking over the past several decades, money can still be made in the right neighborhoods, typically in the suburbs.

On the other hand, there are many rural towns in the county that are dying. Those towns typically are far from a major metropolitan area and typically offer little employment opportunities. Perhaps homes are being abandoned and businesses boarded up. If there is little chance of population growth, it is suggested that perhaps investing in a rental home, or even your own home, may not be a good idea.

Instead, consider investing in the S&P 500 until you decide to move and settle in a more thriving community.

Get Started: Minimize your expenses. Keep track of every dollar you spend. As soon as you have a few thousand dollars saved, open up a high yield money market account for your cash reserves and brokerage account for your stock market investments. Put whatever goes into the brokerage account into an S&P 500 type mutual fund. Charles Schwab, Fidelity, and Vanguard all offer such low-cost funds.

After you have saved enough for a down payment, consider buying a home, but only if you plan to reside in your area for an indefinite period of time. If your job requires you to move frequently, perhaps home ownership is not for you, and you should continue with your S&P500 mutual fund investment plan.

Otherwise start looking at as many homes in your area of interest as possible. Talk to a local lender to get pre-qualified for a loan. Open houses are a good way to familiarize yourself with typical homes in your area.

Ask lots of questions. You can learn more with your ears than you can with your eyes. Make offers at somewhat less than the asking prices. Keep in mind that purchasing your second and third homes will be much easier.

Don't be discouraged by bad news. Prices in both the stock market and the housing market will already reflect those negative expectations. Often the most profitable investments are acquired when the outlook looks bleak!

Consider re-reading at least parts of this book every year of two. The trip of a thousand miles begins with one little step. The principles discussed in this book made a difference in my life and I hope they will make a difference in your life as well.

So get started: A journey of a thousand miles begins with a single step. So, start walking!

***

Appendix A

APPENDIX A
Compound Interest Table - $100 Initial Investment

% Rate	1 Year	5 Years	10 Years	15 Years	20 Years	25 Years	30 Years
1%	101.00	105.10	110.46	116.10	122.02	128.24	134.78
2%	102.00	110.41	121.90	134.59	148.59	164.06	181.14
3%	103.00	115.93	134.39	155.80	180.61	209.38	242.73
4%	104.00	121.67	148.02	180.09	219.11	266.58	324.34
5%	105.00	127.63	162.89	207.89	265.33	338.64	432.19
6%	106.00	133.82	179.08	239.66	320.71	429.19	574.35
7%	107.00	140.26	196.72	275.90	386.97	542.74	761.23
8%	108.00	146.93	215.89	317.22	466.10	684.85	1,006.27
9%	109.00	153.86	236.74	364.25	560.44	862.31	1,326.77
10%	110.00	161.05	259.37	417.72	672.75	1,083.47	1,744.94
11%	111.00	168.51	283.94	478.46	806.23	1,358.55	2,289.23
12%	112.00	176.23	310.58	547.36	964.63	1,700.01	2,995.99
13%	113.00	184.24	339.46	625.43	1,152.31	2,123.05	3,911.59
14%	114.00	192.54	370.72	713.79	1,374.35	2,646.19	5,095.02
15%	115.00	201.14	404.56	813.71	1,636.65	3,291.90	6,621.18
16%	116.00	210.03	441.14	926.55	1,946.08	4,087.42	8,584.99
17%	117.00	219.24	480.68	1,053.87	2,310.56	5,065.78	11,106.47
18%	118.00	228.78	523.38	1,197.37	2,739.30	6,266.86	14,337.06
19%	119.00	238.64	569.47	1,358.95	3,242.94	7,738.81	18,467.53
20%	120.00	248.83	619.17	1,540.70	3,833.76	9,539.62	23,737.63
21%	121.00	259.37	672.75	1,744.94	4,525.93	11,739.09	30,448.16
22%	122.00	270.27	730.46	1,974.23	5,335.76	14,421.01	38,975.79
23%	123.00	281.53	792.59	2,231.40	6,282.06	17,685.93	49,791.29
24%	124.00	293.16	859.44	2,519.56	7,386.41	21,654.20	63,481.99
25%	125.00	305.18	931.32	2,842.17	8,673.62	26,469.78	80,779.36

This table assumes a onetime investment of $100.00 at the beginning of the first year and shows what that initial investment will grow to assuming different compounded rates of interest (the first vertical column on the left) over different time periods (the top horizontal column.)

Here is an example of how to use this table:

John invests $100 at 5%. What will his investment be worth in 10 years? To solve: Look for the intersection above of 5% and 10 years. The answer: $162.89. His total interest, or profit, would be $162.89 less his initial investment of $100, or $62.89.

John makes a $2,000 purchase on his credit card which charges him 24% interest and keeps an unpaid balance on his card of at least the original charge and the accumulated interest. How much will that purchase cost him over 10 years? To solve: Look for the intersection above of 24% and 10 years (859.44). Multiply that times how many $100's are in $2,000, which is 20.

The answer: $859.44 times 20 = $17,188.80. His total interest paid would be $17,188, less his initial loan amount of $2,000, or $15,188.

***

Appendix B

APPENDIX B

Periodic Payments of $100 Compounded Annually

% Rate	1 Year	5 Years	10 Years	15 Years	20 Years	25 Years	30 Years
1%	101.00	515.20	1,056.68	1,625.79	2,223.92	2,852.56	3,513.27
2%	102.00	530.81	1,116.87	1,763.93	2,478.33	3,267.09	4,137.94
3%	103.00	546.84	1,180.78	1,915.69	2,767.65	3,755.30	4,900.27
4%	104.00	563.30	1,248.64	2,082.45	3,096.92	4,331.17	5,832.83
5%	105.00	580.19	1,320.68	2,265.75	3,471.93	5,011.35	6,976.08
6%	106.00	597.53	1,397.16	2,467.25	3,899.27	5,815.64	8,380.17
7%	107.00	615.33	1,478.36	2,688.81	4,386.52	6,767.65	10,107.30
8%	108.00	633.59	1,564.55	2,932.43	4,942.29	7,895.44	12,234.59
9%	109.00	652.33	1,656.03	3,200.34	5,576.45	9,232.40	14,857.52
10%	110.00	671.56	1,753.12	3,494.97	6,300.25	10,818.18	18,094.34
11%	111.00	691.29	1,856.14	3,818.99	7,126.51	12,699.88	22,091.32
12%	112.00	711.52	1,965.46	4,175.33	8,069.87	14,933.39	27,029.26
13%	113.00	732.27	2,081.43	4,567.17	9,146.99	17,585.01	33,131.51
14%	114.00	753.55	2,204.45	4,998.04	10,376.84	20,733.27	40,673.70
15%	115.00	775.37	2,334.93	5,471.75	11,781.01	24,471.20	49,995.69
16%	116.00	797.75	2,473.29	5,992.50	13,384.05	28,908.83	61,516.16
17%	117.00	820.68	2,619.99	6,564.88	15,213.85	34,176.27	75,750.38
18%	118.00	844.20	2,775.51	7,193.90	17,302.10	40,427.21	93,331.86
19%	119.00	868.30	2,940.35	7,885.02	19,684.74	47,843.06	115,038.75
20%	120.00	892.99	3,115.04	8,644.21	22,402.56	56,637.73	141,825.79
21%	121.00	918.30	3,300.13	9,477.99	25,501.76	67,063.30	174,863.23
22%	122.00	944.23	3,496.20	10,393.45	29,034.69	79,416.53	215,583.92
23%	123.00	970.79	3,703.88	11,398.34	33,060.59	94,046.47	265,740.36
24%	124.00	998.01	3,923.79	12,501.08	37,646.48	111,363.36	327,473.63
25%	125.00	1,025.88	4,156.61	13,710.85	42,868.09	131,848.90	403,396.78

This table assumes an investment of $100.00 at the beginning of the each year and shows what those cumulative investments will grow to assuming different rates of interest (the first vertical column on the left) over different time periods (the top horizontal column.)

An example of how to use this table: John invests $100 at the beginning of each year in a 5% savings account. What will his savings account investment be worth in 10 years? To solve: Look for the intersection above of 5% and 10 years. The answer: $1,320.68. His total interest earned would be $1,320.68 less his total investments of $1,000 (10 years of $100 per year), or $320.68.

John charges $500 at the beginning of each year on his credit card more than he repays. His credit card charges him 24% interest, and John keeps an unpaid balance on his card of at least the original charge and the accumulated interest. How much will those annual $500 charges cost him over 15 years?

To solve: Look for the intersection above of 24% and 15 years (12,501.08). Multiply that times how many $100's are in $500, which is 5. The answer: $12,501.08 times 5 = $62,505.40. His total interest paid would be $62,505.40 less his total borrowings of $7,500 (15 times $500), or $55,005.40.

This table can also be used to estimate how much annual dollar amount invested monthly will grow to over a period of time. But because the amount is invested each month, rather than the beginning of each year, it will take approximately an extra six months to accumulate to the indicated value.

For instance, in the above example, if John had charged the annual $500 in equal amounts each month ($41.67 each month), rather than the full amount at beginning of each year, the initial loan and interest would have grown to the $62,505.40 over approximately 15.5 years rather than 15 years. For the sake of simplicity in this book we have used the 15 year value without considering the extra 1/2 year which may be required.

***

Appendix C

APPENDIX C

MONTHLY MORTGAGE PAYMENTS ON A $100,000 LOAN

Rate	5 Years	10 Years	15 Years	20 Years	25 Years	30 Years
3.00%	1,796.87	965.61	690.58	554.60	474.21	421.60
3.25%	1,808.00	977.19	702.67	567.20	487.32	435.21
3.50%	1,819.17	988.86	714.88	579.96	500.62	449.04
3.75%	1,830.39	1,000.61	727.22	592.89	514.13	463.12
4.00%	1,841.65	1,012.45	739.69	605.98	527.84	477.42
4.25%	1,852.96	1,024.38	752.28	619.23	541.74	491.94
4.50%	1,864.30	1,036.38	764.99	632.65	555.83	506.69
4.75%	1,875.69	1,048.48	777.83	546.22	570.12	521.65
5.00%	1,887.12	1,060.66	790.79	659.96	584.59	536.82
5.25%	1,898.60	1,072.92	803.88	673.84	599.25	552.20
5.50%	1,910.12	1,085.26	817.08	687.89	614.09	567.79
5.75%	1,921.68	1,097.69	830.41	702.08	629.11	583.57
6.00%	1,933.28	1,110.21	843.86	716.43	644.30	599.55
6.25%	1,944.93	1,122.80	857.42	730.93	659.67	615.72
6.50%	1,956.61	1,135.48	871.11	745.57	675.21	632.07
6.75%	1,968.35	1,148.24	884.91	760.36	690.91	648.60
7.00%	1,980.12	1,161.08	898.83	775.30	706.78	665.30
7.25%	1,991.94	1,174.01	912.86	790.38	722.81	682.18
7.50%	2,003.79	1,187.02	927.01	805.59	738.99	699.21
7.75%	2,015.70	1,200.11	941.28	820.95	755.33	716.41
8.00%	2,027.64	1,213.28	955.65	836.44	771.82	733.76
8.50%	2,051.65	1,239.86	984.74	867.82	805.23	768.91
9.00%	2,075.84	1,266.76	1,014.27	899.73	839.20	804.62
9.50%	2,100.19	1,293.98	1,044.22	932.13	873.70	840.85
10.00%	2,124.70	1,321.51	1,074.61	965.02	908.70	877.57
11.00%	2,174.24	1,377.50	1,136.60	1,032.19	980.11	952.32
12.00%	2,224.44	1,434.71	1,200.17	1,101.09	1,053.22	1,028.61
13.00%	2,275.31	1,493.11	1,265.24	1,171.58	1,127.84	1,106.20
14.00%	2,326.83	1,552.66	1,331.74	1,243.52	1,203.76	1,184.87
15.00%	2,378.99	1,613.35	1,399.59	1,316.79	1,280.83	1,264.44
16.00%	2,431.81	1,675.13	1,468.70	1,391.26	1,358.89	1,344.76

This table shows the payment required to fully amortize a given loan over different periods of time.

An example of how to use this table: John obtains a $220,000 mortgage at 6% amortized over 30 years. What is his monthly payment of principal and interest?

To solve: Look for the intersection above of 6% and 30 years (599.55). Multiply that times how many $100,000's are in the loan amount of $220,000 (2.2). The answer: $599.55 times 2.2 = $1,319.01 per month.

The actual mortgage payment may be a few hundred dollars more if the lender requires that property taxes and insurance be escrowed. To estimate that additional amount, simply divide the sum of the property taxes (say $2,000) and the property insurance (say $400), by 12.

In this example, the mortgage payment would be increased by $200 per month ($2,400/12), for a total PITI (principal, interest, taxes and insurance) payment of $1,519.01 per month.

On the following pages, I have provided a typical loan amortization, showing the monthly pay down of a $200,000 mortgage amortized over 30 years at 5%..

Loan Amortization Schedule

Principal: 200,000
Monthly Payment: 1,073.64
Loan for Months: 360
Interest Rate: 5.0%

Month	Beginning Principal	Interest Payment	Principal Payment	Ending Principal
1	200,000.00	833.33	240.31	199,759.69
2	199,759.69	832.33	241.31	199,518.38
3	199,518.38	831.33	242.32	199,276.06
4	199,276.06	830.32	243.33	199,032.74
5	199,032.74	829.30	244.34	198,788.40
6	198,788.40	828.28	245.36	198,543.04
7	198,543.04	827.26	246.38	198,296.66
8	198,296.66	826.24	247.41	198,049.25
9	198,049.25	825.21	248.44	197,800.81
10	197,800.81	824.17	249.47	197,551.34
11	197,551.34	823.13	250.51	197,300.83
12	197,300.83	822.09	251.56	197,049.27
13	197,049.27	821.04	252.60	196,796.66
14	196,796.66	819.99	253.66	196,543.01
15	196,543.01	818.93	254.71	196,288.29
16	196,288.29	817.87	255.78	196,032.52
17	196,032.52	816.80	256.84	195,775.68
18	195,775.68	815.73	257.91	195,517.77
19	195,517.77	814.66	258.99	195,258.78
20	195,258.78	813.58	260.06	194,998.71
21	194,998.71	812.49	261.15	194,737.57
22	194,737.57	811.41	262.24	194,475.33
23	194,475.33	810.31	263.33	194,212.00
24	194,212.00	809.22	264.43	193,947.57
25	193,947.57	808.11	265.53	193,682.05
26	193,682.05	807.01	266.63	193,415.41
27	193,415.41	805.90	267.75	193,147.66
28	193,147.66	804.78	268.86	192,878.80
29	192,878.80	803.66	269.98	192,608.82
30	192,608.82	802.54	271.11	192,337.72
31	192,337.72	801.41	272.24	192,065.48
32	192,065.48	800.27	273.37	191,792.11
33	191,792.11	799.13	274.51	191,517.60
34	191,517.60	797.99	275.65	191,241.95
35	191,241.95	796.84	276.80	190,965.14

36	190,965.14	795.69	277.96	190,687.19
37	190,687.19	794.53	279.11	190,408.08
38	190,408.08	793.37	280.28	190,127.80
39	190,127.80	792.20	281.44	189,846.36
40	189,846.36	791.03	282.62	189,563.74
41	189,563.74	789.85	283.79	189,279.94
42	189,279.94	788.67	284.98	188,994.97
43	188,994.97	787.48	286.16	188,708.80
44	188,708.80	786.29	287.36	188,421.45
45	188,421.45	785.09	288.55	188,132.89
46	188,132.89	783.89	289.76	187,843.14
47	187,843.14	782.68	290.96	187,552.17
48	187,552.17	781.47	292.18	187,260.00
49	187,260.00	780.25	293.39	186,966.60
50	186,966.60	779.03	294.62	186,671.99
51	186,671.99	777.80	295.84	186,376.15
52	186,376.15	776.57	297.08	186,079.07
53	186,079.07	775.33	298.31	185,780.76
54	185,780.76	774.09	299.56	185,481.20
55	185,481.20	772.84	300.80	185,180.39
56	185,180.39	771.58	302.06	184,878.34
57	184,878.34	770.33	303.32	184,575.02
58	184,575.02	769.06	304.58	184,270.44
59	184,270.44	767.79	305.85	183,964.59
60	183,964.59	766.52	307.12	183,657.46
61	183,657.46	765.24	308.40	183,349.06
62	183,349.06	763.95	309.69	183,039.37
63	183,039.37	762.66	310.98	182,728.39
64	182,728.39	761.37	312.27	182,416.12
65	182,416.12	760.07	313.58	182,102.54
66	182,102.54	758.76	314.88	181,787.66
67	181,787.66	757.45	316.19	181,471.46
68	181,471.46	756.13	317.51	181,153.95
69	181,153.95	754.81	318.84	180,835.12
70	180,835.12	753.48	320.16	180,514.95
71	180,514.95	752.15	321.50	180,193.46
72	180,193.46	750.81	322.84	179,870.62
73	179,870.62	749.46	324.18	179,546.44
74	179,546.44	748.11	325.53	179,220.90
75	179,220.90	746.75	326.89	178,894.01
76	178,894.01	745.39	328.25	178,565.76
77	178,565.76	744.02	329.62	178,236.14
78	178,236.14	742.65	330.99	177,905.15
79	177,905.15	741.27	332.37	177,572.78
80	177,572.78	739.89	333.76	177,239.02
81	177,239.02	738.50	335.15	176,903.87
82	176,903.87	737.10	336.54	176,567.33

83	176,567.33	735.70	337.95	176,229.38
84	176,229.38	734.29	339.35	175,890.03
85	175,890.03	732.88	340.77	175,549.26
86	175,549.26	731.46	342.19	175,207.07
87	175,207.07	730.03	343.61	174,863.46
88	174,863.46	728.60	345.05	174,518.41
89	174,518.41	727.16	346.48	174,171.93
90	174,171.93	725.72	347.93	173,824.00
91	173,824.00	724.27	349.38	173,474.63
92	173,474.63	722.81	350.83	173,123.80
93	173,123.80	721.35	352.29	172,771.50
94	172,771.50	719.88	353.76	172,417.74
95	172,417.74	718.41	355.24	172,062.50
96	172,062.50	716.93	356.72	171,705.79
97	171,705.79	715.44	358.20	171,347.59
98	171,347.59	713.95	359.69	170,987.89
99	170,987.89	712.45	361.19	170,626.70
100	170,626.70	710.94	362.70	170,264.00
101	170,264.00	709.43	364.21	169,899.79
102	169,899.79	707.92	365.73	169,534.06
103	169,534.06	706.39	367.25	169,166.81
104	169,166.81	704.86	368.78	168,798.03
105	168,798.03	703.33	370.32	168,427.71
106	168,427.71	701.78	371.86	168,055.85
107	168,055.85	700.23	373.41	167,682.44
108	167,682.44	698.68	374.97	167,307.47
109	167,307.47	697.11	376.53	166,930.94
110	166,930.94	695.55	378.10	166,552.85
111	166,552.85	693.97	379.67	166,173.17
112	166,173.17	692.39	381.26	165,791.92
113	165,791.92	690.80	382.84	165,409.07
114	165,409.07	689.20	384.44	165,024.63
115	165,024.63	687.60	386.04	164,638.59
116	164,638.59	685.99	387.65	164,250.94
117	164,250.94	684.38	389.26	163,861.68
118	163,861.68	682.76	390.89	163,470.79
119	163,470.79	681.13	392.51	163,078.28
120	163,078.28	679.49	394.15	162,684.13
121	162,684.13	677.85	395.79	162,288.34
122	162,288.34	676.20	397.44	161,890.89
123	161,890.89	674.55	399.10	161,491.80
124	161,491.80	672.88	400.76	161,091.04
125	161,091.04	671.21	402.43	160,688.61
126	160,688.61	669.54	404.11	160,284.50
127	160,284.50	667.85	405.79	159,878.71
128	159,878.71	666.16	407.48	159,471.22
129	159,471.22	664.46	409.18	159,062.04

130	159,062.04	662.76	410.88	158,651.16
131	158,651.16	661.05	412.60	158,238.56
132	158,238.56	659.33	414.32	157,824.25
133	157,824.25	657.60	416.04	157,408.21
134	157,408.21	655.87	417.78	156,990.43
135	156,990.43	654.13	419.52	156,570.91
136	156,570.91	652.38	421.26	156,149.65
137	156,149.65	650.62	423.02	155,726.63
138	155,726.63	648.86	424.78	155,301.85
139	155,301.85	647.09	426.55	154,875.29
140	154,875.29	645.31	428.33	154,446.96
141	154,446.96	643.53	430.11	154,016.85
142	154,016.85	641.74	431.91	153,584.94
143	153,584.94	639.94	433.71	153,151.24
144	153,151.24	638.13	435.51	152,715.73
145	152,715.73	636.32	437.33	152,278.40
146	152,278.40	634.49	439.15	151,839.25
147	151,839.25	632.66	440.98	151,398.27
148	151,398.27	630.83	442.82	150,955.45
149	150,955.45	628.98	444.66	150,510.79
150	150,510.79	627.13	446.51	150,064.27
151	150,064.27	625.27	448.38	149,615.90
152	149,615.90	623.40	450.24	149,165.65
153	149,165.65	621.52	452.12	148,713.53
154	148,713.53	619.64	454.00	148,259.53
155	148,259.53	617.75	455.90	147,803.64
156	147,803.64	615.85	457.79	147,345.84
157	147,345.84	613.94	459.70	146,886.14
158	146,886.14	612.03	461.62	146,424.52
159	146,424.52	610.10	463.54	145,960.98
160	145,960.98	608.17	465.47	145,495.51
161	145,495.51	606.23	467.41	145,028.10
162	145,028.10	604.28	469.36	144,558.74
163	144,558.74	602.33	471.32	144,087.42
164	144,087.42	600.36	473.28	143,614.14
165	143,614.14	598.39	475.25	143,138.89
166	143,138.89	596.41	477.23	142,661.66
167	142,661.66	594.42	479.22	142,182.44
168	142,182.44	592.43	481.22	141,701.22
169	141,701.22	590.42	483.22	141,218.00
170	141,218.00	588.41	485.23	140,732.77
171	140,732.77	586.39	487.26	140,245.51
172	140,245.51	584.36	489.29	139,756.22
173	139,756.22	582.32	491.33	139,264.90
174	139,264.90	580.27	493.37	138,771.53
175	138,771.53	578.21	495.43	138,276.10
176	138,276.10	576.15	497.49	137,778.60

177	137,778.60	574.08	499.57	137,279.04
178	137,279.04	572.00	501.65	136,777.39
179	136,777.39	569.91	503.74	136,273.65
180	136,273.65	567.81	505.84	135,767.82
181	135,767.82	565.70	507.94	135,259.87
182	135,259.87	563.58	510.06	134,749.81
183	134,749.81	561.46	512.19	134,237.63
184	134,237.63	559.32	514.32	133,723.31
185	133,723.31	557.18	516.46	133,206.84
186	133,206.84	555.03	518.61	132,688.23
187	132,688.23	552.87	520.78	132,167.45
188	132,167.45	550.70	522.95	131,644.51
189	131,644.51	548.52	525.12	131,119.38
190	131,119.38	546.33	527.31	130,592.07
191	130,592.07	544.13	529.51	130,062.56
192	130,062.56	541.93	531.72	129,530.85
193	129,530.85	539.71	533.93	128,996.91
194	128,996.91	537.49	536.16	128,460.76
195	128,460.76	535.25	538.39	127,922.37
196	127,922.37	533.01	540.63	127,381.74
197	127,381.74	530.76	542.89	126,838.85
198	126,838.85	528.50	545.15	126,293.70
199	126,293.70	526.22	547.42	125,746.28
200	125,746.28	523.94	549.70	125,196.58
201	125,196.58	521.65	551.99	124,644.59
202	124,644.59	519.35	554.29	124,090.30
203	124,090.30	517.04	556.60	123,533.70
204	123,533.70	514.72	558.92	122,974.78
205	122,974.78	512.39	561.25	122,413.53
206	122,413.53	510.06	563.59	121,849.94
207	121,849.94	507.71	565.94	121,284.01
208	121,284.01	505.35	568.29	120,715.72
209	120,715.72	502.98	570.66	120,145.06
210	120,145.06	500.60	573.04	119,572.02
211	119,572.02	498.22	575.43	118,996.59
212	118,996.59	495.82	577.82	118,418.77
213	118,418.77	493.41	580.23	117,838.53
214	117,838.53	490.99	582.65	117,255.88
215	117,255.88	488.57	585.08	116,670.81
216	116,670.81	486.13	587.51	116,083.29
217	116,083.29	483.68	589.96	115,493.33
218	115,493.33	481.22	592.42	114,900.91
219	114,900.91	478.75	594.89	114,306.02
220	114,306.02	476.28	597.37	113,708.65
221	113,708.65	473.79	599.86	113,108.79
222	113,108.79	471.29	602.36	112,506.44
223	112,506.44	468.78	604.87	111,901.57

224	111,901.57	466.26	607.39	111,294.18
225	111,294.18	463.73	609.92	110,684.27
226	110,684.27	461.18	612.46	110,071.81
227	110,071.81	458.63	615.01	109,456.80
228	109,456.80	456.07	617.57	108,839.22
229	108,839.22	453.50	620.15	108,219.08
230	108,219.08	450.91	622.73	107,596.35
231	107,596.35	448.32	625.33	106,971.02
232	106,971.02	445.71	627.93	106,343.09
233	106,343.09	443.10	630.55	105,712.54
234	105,712.54	440.47	633.17	105,079.37
235	105,079.37	437.83	635.81	104,443.56
236	104,443.56	435.18	638.46	103,805.10
237	103,805.10	432.52	641.12	103,163.97
238	103,163.97	429.85	643.79	102,520.18
239	102,520.18	427.17	646.48	101,873.70
240	101,873.70	424.47	649.17	101,224.54
241	101,224.54	421.77	651.87	100,572.66
242	100,572.66	419.05	654.59	99,918.07
243	99,918.07	416.33	657.32	99,260.75
244	99,260.75	413.59	660.06	98,600.70
245	98,600.70	410.84	662.81	97,937.89
246	97,937.89	408.07	665.57	97,272.32
247	97,272.32	405.30	668.34	96,603.98
248	96,603.98	402.52	671.13	95,932.85
249	95,932.85	399.72	673.92	95,258.93
250	95,258.93	396.91	676.73	94,582.20
251	94,582.20	394.09	679.55	93,902.65
252	93,902.65	391.26	682.38	93,220.26
253	93,220.26	388.42	685.23	92,535.04
254	92,535.04	385.56	688.08	91,846.96
255	91,846.96	382.70	690.95	91,156.01
256	91,156.01	379.82	693.83	90,462.18
257	90,462.18	376.93	696.72	89,765.47
258	89,765.47	374.02	699.62	89,065.85
259	89,065.85	371.11	702.54	88,363.31
260	88,363.31	368.18	705.46	87,657.85
261	87,657.85	365.24	708.40	86,949.45
262	86,949.45	362.29	711.35	86,238.09
263	86,238.09	359.33	714.32	85,523.77
264	85,523.77	356.35	717.29	84,806.48
265	84,806.48	353.36	720.28	84,086.20
266	84,086.20	350.36	723.28	83,362.91
267	83,362.91	347.35	726.30	82,636.61
268	82,636.61	344.32	729.32	81,907.29
269	81,907.29	341.28	732.36	81,174.93
270	81,174.93	338.23	735.41	80,439.51

271	80,439.51	335.16	738.48	79,701.03
272	79,701.03	332.09	741.56	78,959.48
273	78,959.48	329.00	744.65	78,214.83
274	78,214.83	325.90	747.75	77,467.09
275	77,467.09	322.78	750.86	76,716.22
276	76,716.22	319.65	753.99	75,962.23
277	75,962.23	316.51	757.13	75,205.10
278	75,205.10	313.35	760.29	74,444.81
279	74,444.81	310.19	763.46	73,681.35
280	73,681.35	307.01	766.64	72,914.71
281	72,914.71	303.81	769.83	72,144.88
282	72,144.88	300.60	773.04	71,371.84
283	71,371.84	297.38	776.26	70,595.58
284	70,595.58	294.15	779.49	69,816.09
285	69,816.09	290.90	782.74	69,033.34
286	69,033.34	287.64	786.00	68,247.34
287	68,247.34	284.36	789.28	67,458.06
288	67,458.06	281.08	792.57	66,665.49
289	66,665.49	277.77	795.87	65,869.62
290	65,869.62	274.46	799.19	65,070.43
291	65,070.43	271.13	802.52	64,267.92
292	64,267.92	267.78	805.86	63,462.06
293	63,462.06	264.43	809.22	62,652.84
294	62,652.84	261.05	812.59	61,840.25
295	61,840.25	257.67	815.98	61,024.27
296	61,024.27	254.27	819.38	60,204.90
297	60,204.90	250.85	822.79	59,382.11
298	59,382.11	247.43	826.22	58,555.89
299	58,555.89	243.98	829.66	57,726.23
300	57,726.23	240.53	833.12	56,893.11
301	56,893.11	237.05	836.59	56,056.53
302	56,056.53	233.57	840.07	55,216.45
303	55,216.45	230.07	843.57	54,372.88
304	54,372.88	226.55	847.09	53,525.79
305	53,525.79	223.02	850.62	52,675.17
306	52,675.17	219.48	854.16	51,821.00
307	51,821.00	215.92	857.72	50,963.28
308	50,963.28	212.35	861.30	50,101.99
309	50,101.99	208.76	864.88	49,237.10
310	49,237.10	205.15	868.49	48,368.61
311	48,368.61	201.54	872.11	47,496.50
312	47,496.50	197.90	875.74	46,620.76
313	46,620.76	194.25	879.39	45,741.37
314	45,741.37	190.59	883.05	44,858.32
315	44,858.32	186.91	886.73	43,971.59
316	43,971.59	183.21	890.43	43,081.16
317	43,081.16	179.50	894.14	42,187.02

318	42,187.02	175.78	897.86	41,289.15
319	41,289.15	172.04	901.61	40,387.55
320	40,387.55	168.28	905.36	39,482.19
321	39,482.19	164.51	909.13	38,573.05
322	38,573.05	160.72	912.92	37,660.13
323	37,660.13	156.92	916.73	36,743.41
324	36,743.41	153.10	920.55	35,822.86
325	35,822.86	149.26	924.38	34,898.48
326	34,898.48	145.41	928.23	33,970.25
327	33,970.25	141.54	932.10	33,038.15
328	33,038.15	137.66	935.98	32,102.16
329	32,102.16	133.76	939.88	31,162.28
330	31,162.28	129.84	943.80	30,218.48
331	30,218.48	125.91	947.73	29,270.74
332	29,270.74	121.96	951.68	28,319.06
333	28,319.06	118.00	955.65	27,363.41
334	27,363.41	114.01	959.63	26,403.79
335	26,403.79	110.02	963.63	25,440.16
336	25,440.16	106.00	967.64	24,472.52
337	24,472.52	101.97	971.67	23,500.84
338	23,500.84	97.92	975.72	22,525.12
339	22,525.12	93.85	979.79	21,545.33
340	21,545.33	89.77	983.87	20,561.46
341	20,561.46	85.67	987.97	19,573.49
342	19,573.49	81.56	992.09	18,581.40
343	18,581.40	77.42	996.22	17,585.18
344	17,585.18	73.27	1,000.37	16,584.81
345	16,584.81	69.10	1,004.54	15,580.27
346	15,580.27	64.92	1,008.73	14,571.54
347	14,571.54	60.71	1,012.93	13,558.61
348	13,558.61	56.49	1,017.15	12,541.47
349	12,541.47	52.26	1,021.39	11,520.08
350	11,520.08	48.00	1,025.64	10,494.44
351	10,494.44	43.73	1,029.92	9,464.52
352	9,464.52	39.44	1,034.21	8,430.31
353	8,430.31	35.13	1,038.52	7,391.79
354	7,391.79	30.80	1,042.84	6,348.95
355	6,348.95	26.45	1,047.19	5,301.76
356	5,301.76	22.09	1,051.55	4,250.21
357	4,250.21	17.71	1,055.93	3,194.27
358	3,194.27	13.31	1,060.33	2,133.94
359	2,133.94	8.89	1,064.75	1,069.19
360	1,069.19	4.45	1,069.19	0.00

.

www.ingramcontent.com/pod-product-compliance
Lightning Source LLC
Chambersburg PA
CBHW071539200326
41519CB00021BB/6550